At Issue

Is Organic Food Better?

Other Books in the At Issue Series:

At Issue

Is Organic Food Better?

Ronald D. Lankford, Jr., Book Editor

GREENHAVEN PRESS
A part of Gale, Cengage Learning

 GALE
CENGAGE Learning

Detroit • New York • San Francisco • New Haven, Conn • Waterville, Maine • London

Christine Nasso, *Publisher*
Elizabeth Des Chenes, *Managing Editor*

For more information, contact:
Greenhaven Press
27500 Drake Rd.
Farmington Hills, MI 48331-3535
Or you can visit our Internet site at gale.cengage.com

For product information and technology assistance, contact us at

Gale Customer Support, 1-800-877-4253
For permission to use material from this text or product, submit all requests online at www.cengage.com/permissions.

Further permissions questions can be e-mailed to permissionrequest@cengage.com.

Articles in Greenhaven Press anthologies are often edited for length to meet page requirements. In addition, original titles of these works are changed to clearly present the main thesis and to explicitly indicate the author's opinion. Every effort is made to ensure that Greenhaven Press accurately reflects the original intent of the authors. Every effort has been made to trace the owners of copyrighted material.

Cover image copyright Debra Hughes 2007. Used under license from Shutterstock.com.

LIBRARY OF CONGRESS CATALOGING-IN-PUBLICATION DATA

Is organic food better? / Ronald D. Lankford, book editor.
    p. cm. -- (At issue)
  Includes bibliographical references and index.
  ISBN 978-0-7377-5157-4 (hardcover) -- ISBN 978-0-7377-5158-1 (pbk.)
  1. Natural foods. 2. Natural foods industry. I. Lankford, Ronald D., 1962- II. Series: At issue (San Diego, Calif.)
  HD9000.5.I814 2011
  641.3'02--dc22

                                                                2011000871

Printed in the United States of America
    1 2 3 4 5   15 14 13 12 11

ED084

Contents

Introduction

In recent years, organic food has generally become more popular, increasing its market share against traditional food sold in discount grocery stores (like Safeway or Kroger). This growth has been evident in the increase of chain stores such as Whole Foods, Earth Fare, and Trader Joe's that specialize in organic products, but also in the decisions of more mainstream grocers like Wal-Mart to carry organic food. The rise in importance of organic food is also evident in the increased involvement of federal agencies like the United States Food and Drug Administration (FDA) in regulating organic food. With a growing customer base, wider availability, and official regulators, many observers believe that organic food will continue to become increasingly popular in the future.

The number of organic food offerings, however, is inequitable with the choices offered in traditional food markets. While there may be multiple reasons for this, one is cited most often: organic food is generally more expensive than traditional, non-organic food. The extra expense of organic food becomes even more problematic during difficult economic times, as with the economic downturn in the United States and Europe that began in 2007. When consumers who are inclined to purchase organic food have less money, they can save by switching to non-organic.

Because of the worldwide recession, social commentators have wondered whether recent trends in organic food sales will be maintained or reversed. Will organic food reach a greater number of consumers in the near future? Or will organic food, as long as it remains more expensive, never reach more than a limited niche group?

Market Shares for Organic Food

According to the Organic Trade Association, organic food purchases have trended upward since 2000. Between 2000 and

2009, sales of organic food in the United States grew from one billion dollars to nearly $25 billion. This increase is also reflected in the amount of land reserved for organic agriculture, equaling 4.8 million acres of crop land and pasture in 2009. According to the Organic Trade Association, sales increased 5.1 percent from 2008 to 2009. While these statistics are impressive evidence of the growth of the organic food market, they should be measured against other organic food trends and changes.

Even as organic food sales grow, they remain a small part of the overall market share in the United States. Organic food and beverages equaled 3.7 percent of the nation's sales on these types of items, while organic farm land equaled only .7 percent of all American farmland. Likewise, organic pasture for livestock only equaled .5 percent of all American pasture. Even while organic food continued to reach more consumers, then, it captured a relatively small portion of the overall market.

In Great Britain, both the land used by organic farmers and the number of organic producers decreased slightly between 2008 and 2009. On the international level, sales of organic food increased by 1.7 percent. While this last statistic shows an increase in the organic food market, it is a significant drop from the 26 percent growth in organic food sales registered over the last several years. This drop suggests that the overall growth of organic food sales on an international level has—at least temporarily—stalled.

Specialty Grocers and Co-ops

The organic food market has experienced other changes and setbacks over the last two or three years. During the recent economic downturn, some specialty grocery stores have lost sales to more mainstream grocers like Safeway and Harris Teeter. This seems to indicate that while a number of consumers continue to buy organic food, they tend to purchase those foods at discount grocery stores rather than specialty stores in a less robust economy. In 2009, for instance, sales at natural food stores had dropped at least 12% from the previous year.

Traditional natural-organic grocery stores have also lost ground to increasingly popular co-ops. With co-ops, a number of people buy-in to a grocery store for a set price, allowing them to own and operate the store. Co-ops specializing in organic food frequently attempt to buy products locally. While co-ops typically only serve a small number of customers (the people who own the store), these stores have less overhead and can provide organic food cheaper than many chain stores. As a result, many people have started local co-ops as a way to avoid the higher costs of grocery chains.

While economic setbacks and co-ops have offered significant challenges to natural food chains like Trader Joe's and Whole Foods, these specialty companies have nonetheless continued to stay profitable and build new stores during the current economic slump. Unlike many traditional grocery chains, they have also been able to remain profitable without cutting prices.

Wave of the Future or Small Niche?

As the growth of organic food markets has slowed, observers have debated the reasons for this slowdown. A key reason is the ongoing economic crisis, squeezing consumers who formerly chose to buy organic food. According to this line of thought, organic food sales will resume growth and steadily increase market share once the US and other world economies begin to recover. It is also possible that current trends, such as the growth of co-ops, will pose less prominent competition.

Others have suggested that organic food levels will remain fairly steady, continuing to capture a niche market of upper middle class consumers, but little more. In other words, these critics have suggested that organic food has reached as many people as it can reach as long as the cost of these products remains significantly higher than traditional groceries. In fact, the argument states, affluent customers are the very reason that the organic market has remained steady during the recent economic downturn: these upper middle class customers have been less affected by the crisis than those with lower incomes.

Other changes, however, may point to future areas of new growth. Companies have begun offering organic baby food and organic pet food, potentially expanding sales to new customers or expanding sales to current customers. How these new products or other trends will affect the organic food market, however, will probably remain unclear until the current economic crisis passes.

1

Organic Food: An Overview

Katherine J. Chen

Katherine J. Chen is a writer majoring in English at Princeton University.

Organic food has become a worldwide trend. While debate continues on whether or not organic food is healthier than non-organic food, consumers find a number of benefits to organic food. For instance, organic vegetables are grown without pesticides, and animals on organic farms are allowed to graze in a natural environment. Also, many consumers believe that organic food tastes better. Despite these advantages, there are problems with organic food from a consumer's point of view. Standards for organic foods are sometimes confusing and many shoppers complain that organic food is too expensive. Despite these outstanding issues, consumers continue to purchase more and more organic food.

The purchase of organic food has become nothing short of a global trend, as consumers aim to spend money on products they feel they can relate to and trust. This means knowing exactly what food is made of, how it is processed and its country of origin.

While millions of shoppers continue to flock to grocery stores and farmers' markets, investing their faith (and dollars) in the promise of healthy organic foods, the debate surrounding the true value of "organic" has yet to reach a definitive conclusion. The return to a so-called "natural diet" piques

Katherine J. Chen, "How Organic Is Organic Food?" *Earth 911*, March 8, 2010. Reprinted with permission.

shoppers' interests—enough to generate a global organic market valued at an estimated $48 billion in 2007.

Is Organic Food Healthier?

In July 2009, researchers in London claimed that customers only purchase organic food because they believe it is healthier for their bodies. Scientists at the London School of Hygiene & Tropical Medicine, however, were not convinced.

After a review of 162 scientific papers published in the last 50 years, the research team concluded that there was simply no notable difference between reportedly healthier organic food and conventionally processed food products.

"There is currently no evidence to support the selection of organically over conventionally produced foods on the basis of nutritional superiority," says Alan Dangour, one of the report's authors.

On the other side of the debate, the Soil Association, an international charity whose primary activities involve campaigning for public education on nutrition and health and participates in the certification of organic food in the U.K., disagrees.

In order to make educated decisions about the benefits of organic food, shoppers must first understand what sets organic products apart.

In response to the July 2009 report on the lack of additional health benefits in organic food, the Soil Association's Policy Director Peter Melchett stated in a press release, "We are disappointed in the conclusions the researchers have reached. The review rejected almost all of the existing studies of comparisons between organic and non-organic nutritional differences."

"Although the researchers say that the differences between organic and non-organic food are not 'important', due to the relatively few studies, they report in their analysis that there are higher levels of beneficial nutrients in organic compared to non-organic foods."

Despite in which camp your opinions lie, the implied power of eating organic still holds sway over shoppers' decisions.

What Does the Label Mean?

In order to make educated decisions about the benefits of organic food, shoppers must first understand what sets organic products apart from their conventional counterparts and what qualifies as "organic" in the U.S.

"Organic refers to the way agricultural products are grown and processed," says Jennifer Rose, new media manager and staff writer of the Organic Trade Association (OTA). "It includes a system of production, processing, distribution and sales that assures consumers that the products maintain the organic integrity that begins on the farm."

"This system which is governed by strict government standards," Rose explains, "requires that products bearing the organic label are made without the use of toxic and persistent pesticides and synthetic nitrogen fertilizers, antibiotics, synthetic hormones, genetic engineering or other excluded practices, sewage, sludge or irradiation."

Jack Hunter, spokesman for the U.K.-based Soil Association, says, "Certain standards for animal welfare, avoidance of chemicals and harmful food additives form the basis for the trade term 'organic.' This is enshrined in European law, but many organizations set their standards above this level, including ours. The Soil Association is considered one of the highest standards in the world, so consumers seeing our distinctive logo can be sure of high standards, policed by our inspectors who visit all levels of the production chain on an annual and unannounced basis."

According to Hunter, many of the benefits of organic food are even overlooked by consumers who believe that these products are better only in the sense that they contain no chemicals, antibiotics, traces of pesticides or fertilizers.

"Organic is a package of really worthwhile things," he says. "This often makes it hard to understand and is why most people think organic equals no chemicals. Organic is all about producing food in a way that doesn't harm people or the environment."

Given the environmental benefits of eating organic, it is no shock that many consumers find organic food more pleasing to the palate.

Sustainable Farming

Organic food is tied directly to the concept of sustainable farming, which covers every part of the food production process from the way animals are fed and their living conditions to the types of amendments that can or cannot be added to the soil in which products are grown.

"So where a worrying amount of pigs, chickens and cows can be reared in miserable conditions, grow faster than their bodies can cope with, are fed things they have not evolved to eat and get a liberal dose of drugs, organic farming does not allow such abuses in the name of profit," Hunter says.

Rose shares a similar sentiment on the overall benefits of organic farming and says that in addition to the environmental benefits, which include soil health, carbon sequestration, clean water supplies and the many personal health advantages organic food has to offer, organic farmers are required by law in the U.S. to "provide their animals with access to the outdoors and pasture, quality organic feed and safe, clean living conditions" without the use of antibiotics or synthetic growth hormones.

"Because organic farms are less intensive, they are far better for wildlife, both in terms of diversity and sheer numbers," Hunter says. "Fields growing wheat one year will need to replace the lost nitrogen through manure and growing clover, for example."

Given the environmental benefits of eating organic, it is no shock either that many consumers find organic food more pleasing to the palate. Nutritionists around the world have also revealed that organic food contains higher levels of several important vitamins and minerals, including vitamin C, calcium, magnesium, iron, and chromium, in addition to cancer-fighting antioxidants and omega-3 fatty acids. According to Hunter, a good example is organic milk, which has on average 68 percent more omega-3 essential fatty acids than conventionally produced milk.

Organic Food Standards

Despite the progressive move towards organic products around the world, there are still some confusing aspects of organic food, such as why standards vary from country to country and also—from an ecological point of view—whether organic food outweighs the benefits of buying local, conventionally grown food from community farmers.

Rose explains that the difference in organic standards exists simply because the development of these laws originates at the national versus international level.

Despite the progressive move towards organic products around the world, there are still some confusing aspects of organic food.

"Some may be very similar as they may have followed direction from an international body, such as the International Federation of Organic Agriculture Movements (IFOAM)," she says. "OTA is supportive of equivalence or trade agreements with other countries, and there has been some progress on this front, such as the equivalence agreement between the U.S. and Canada signed last year [2009]."

"However, in order to be sold as organic in the U.S., products, regardless of their origin, must meet U.S. standards. Thus, it doesn't matter where they were grown. They must be certified by USDA [United States Department of Agriculture] accredited certifying agents or by agencies within their countries that have been recognized by USDA as meeting the requirements of the National Organic Program."

When asked which is more beneficial, buying local produce from farmers or purchasing organic food from the supermarket, Rose says, "It's great if you have a personal relationship with a local farmer whose production methods you can trust. It is important to remember, though, that only products bearing the organic label afford government-backed assurance about how they were grown and processed. So, if you want to be sure that what you buy has indeed been grown and processed according to strict production and processing standards, organic is the best choice."

When it comes to organic foods, sentiments and opinions run strong.

Organic Food's Carbon Footprint

Hunter, on the other hand, advises consumers to do a little bit of both when grocery shopping.

"Local food is going to be fresher than anything you can buy in the supermarket, organic or not," he says. "Because many nutrients break down with time, local food is often more nutritious, too. But unless it's organic, it may have been grown with pesticides and on farms that are a disaster for wildlife. If you can afford it, buy local and organic. Often, local is the cheapest way of buying organic. It's significantly cheaper to get through box schemes than at the supermarket and sometimes even cheaper at a farm shop or farmers' market."

Yet another issue that researchers have raised in the past is whether or not the benefits of organic food outweigh the extra costs in shipping or fuel. In terms of fossil fuels, is an organic apple traveling from Washington state to Pennsylvania really worth the extra mileage?

Rose says organic food actually helps to reduce our carbon footprint and combat climate change by preventing organic farmers from using fossil fuel-based fertilizers. She believes that shipping organic products, even from a distance as wide as California to New York, makes no difference since non-organic products are usually shipped the same way.

Hunter, however, sees it differently. "The benefits and pitfalls of flying produce around the world is a complicated one involving third world development, consumer choice and the balancing of competing environmental issues," he says. "Some products can't be grown in colder climates and need to be transported long distances. This isn't much of an issue where these are shipped, but are problematic when flying is involved. Some of this is undoubtedly organic."

Is Non-Organic Food Really Cheaper?

When it comes to organic foods, sentiments and opinions run strong. While researchers such as those at the London School of Hygiene & Tropical Medicine believe that the alleged benefits of organic food are negligible, other organizations are campaigning in countries around the world to promote the consumption of organic produce and meat.

"The basic message is that in the race to make food cheap—which is a good thing—there has been these unintended consequences which mean that really, it's not that cheap at all," Hunter says. "Not if you consider that so many of us are becoming obese, in large part because of the rubbish many of us are now eating. It's also not cheap on the animals that suffer or the environment that is trashed."

Whatever the opinion of these organizations or campaigns, the ultimate choice is still left to the consumer, who must determine whether the extra financial costs of organic food are worth the health benefits so frequently debated by researchers for nearly an entire century.

2

National Standards for Organic Food

United States Department of Agriculture

The United States Department of Agriculture (USDA) oversees farm product standards by conducting inspections and enforcing federal laws. The USDA's oversight includes the development and implementation of the National Organic Program.

In 1990, Congress passed an organic food act, allowing the USDA to regulate organic farms and organic food standards. These standards include setting criteria for production and handling, labeling, certification, and accreditation of organic products. While these standards are designed to regulate domestic organic food production, they also apply to any imported organic food.

Congress passed the Organic Foods Production Act (OFPA) of 1990. The OFPA required the U.S. Department of Agriculture (USDA) to develop national standards for organically produced agricultural products to assure consumers that agricultural products marketed as organic meet consistent, uniform standards. The OFPA and the National Organic Program (NOP) regulations require that agricultural products labeled as organic originate from farms or handling operations certified by a State or private entity that has been accredited by USDA.

The NOP is a marketing program housed within the USDA Agricultural Marketing Service. Neither the OFPA nor the NOP regulations address food safety or nutrition.

USDA, "National Organic Program," April 2008. Reprinted with permission.

How Was the NOP Developed?

The NOP developed national organic standards and established an organic certification program based on recommendations of the 15-member National Organic Standards Board (NOSB). The NOSB is appointed by the Secretary of Agriculture and is comprised of representatives from the following categories: farmer/grower; handler/processor; retailer; consumer/public interest; environmentalist; scientist; and certifying agent.

Organic crops are raised without using most conventional pesticides, petroleum-based fertilizers, or sewage sludge-based fertilizers.

In addition to considering NOSB recommendations, USDA reviewed State, private and foreign organic certification programs to help formulate these regulations. The NOP regulations are flexible enough to accommodate the wide range of operations and products grown and raised in every region of the United States.

What Is in the NOP Regulations?

Production and handling standards address organic crop production, wild crop harvesting, organic livestock management, and processing and handling of organic agricultural products. Organic crops are raised without using most conventional pesticides, petroleum-based fertilizers, or sewage sludge-based fertilizers. Animals raised on an organic operation must be fed organic feed and given access to the outdoors. They are given no antibiotics or growth hormones.

The NOP regulations prohibit the use of genetic engineering, ionizing radiation, and sewage sludge in organic production and handling. As a general rule, all natural (non-synthetic) substances are allowed in organic production and all synthetic substances are prohibited. The National List of Allowed Synthetic and Prohibited Non-Synthetic Substances, a section in the regulations, contains the specific exceptions to the rule.

Labeling standards are based on the percentage of organic ingredients in a product. Products labeled "100 percent organic" must contain only organically produced ingredients. Products labeled "organic" must consist of at least 95 percent organically produced ingredients. Products meeting the requirements for "100 percent organic" and "organic" may display the USDA Organic seal.

Products labeled "100 percent organic" must contain only organically produced ingredients.

Processed products that contain at least 70 percent organic ingredients can use the phrase "made with organic ingredients" and list up to three of the organic ingredients or food groups on the principal display panel. For example, soup made with at least 70 percent organic ingredients and only organic vegetables may be labeled either "made with organic peas, potatoes, and carrots," or "made with organic vegetables." The USDA Organic seal cannot be used anywhere on the package.

Processed products that contain less than 70 percent organic ingredients cannot use the term "organic" other than to identify the specific ingredients that are organically produced in the ingredients statement.

A civil penalty of up to $11,000 for each offense can be levied on any person who knowingly sells or labels as organic a product that is not produced and handled in accordance with the National Organic Program's regulations.

Certification standards establish the requirements that organic production and handling operations must meet to become accredited by USDA-accredited certifying agents. The information that an applicant must submit to the certifying agent includes the applicant's organic system plan. This plan describes (among other things) practices and substances used in production, record keeping procedures, and practices to prevent commingling of organic and non-organic products. The certification standards also address on-site inspections.

Producers and handling (processing) operations that sell less than $5,000 a year in organic agricultural products are exempt from certification. They may label their products organic if they abide by the standards, but they cannot display the USDA Organic seal. Retail operations, such as grocery stores and restaurants, do not have to be certified.

Accreditation standards establish the requirements an applicant must meet in order to become a USDA-accredited certifying agent. The standards are designed to ensure that all organic certifying agents act consistently and impartially. Successful applicants will employ experienced personnel, demonstrate their expertise in certifying organic producers and handlers, and prevent conflicts of interest and maintain strict confidentiality.

Imported agricultural products may be sold in the United States if they are certified by USDA-accredited certifying agents. Imported products must meet the NOP standards. USDA has accredited certifying agents in several foreign countries.

In lieu [instead] of USDA accreditation, a foreign entity also may be accredited when USDA "recognizes" that its government is able to assess and accredit certifying agents as meeting the requirements of the NOP—called a recognition agreement.

3

Consumers Should Not Support Organic Foods

Rob Johnston

Rob Johnston is a doctor and science writer.

While organic food is a popular trend, many of its supposed benefits are myths. It is assumed, for instance, that organic food is good for the environment and creates sustainable agriculture. In truth, organic produce and livestock often require more carbon energy to sustain production than standard agriculture. Likewise, organic farmers declare that they do not use pesticides, but nonetheless use non-degradable copper-based solutions to treat funguses. There is also no evidence that organic food is healthier or more nutritious than non-organic food. In fact, even the belief that organic food is becoming more popular is false. In truth, less farm land is being used for organic agriculture today than in 2003.

Myth One: Organic Farming Is Good for the Environment

The study of Life Cycle Assessments (LCAs)[1] for the UK, sponsored by the Department for Environment, Food and Rural Affairs, should concern anyone who buys organic. It shows that milk and dairy production is a major source of greenhouse gas emissions (GHGs). A litre of organic milk requires

1. A Life Cycle Assessment determines the possible environmental impact of a product, process or service.

Rob Johnston, "The Great Organic Myths," *Independent*, May 2008. Reprinted by permission.

80 percent more land than conventional milk to produce, has 20 percent greater global warming potential, releases 60 percent more nutrients to water sources, and contributes 70 percent more to acid rain.

Also, organically reared cows burp twice as much methane as conventionally reared cattle—and methane is 20 times more powerful a greenhouse gas than CO_2 [carbon dioxide]. Meat and poultry are the largest agricultural contributors to GHG emissions. LCA assessment counts the energy used to manufacture pesticide for growing cattle feed, but still shows that a kilo of organic beef releases 12 percent more GHGs, causes twice as much nutrient pollution and more acid rain.

Life Cycle Assessment (LCA) relates food production to: energy required to manufacture artificial fertilisers and pesticides; fossil fuel burnt by farm equipment; nutrient pollution caused by nitrate and phosphate run-off into water courses; release of gases that cause acid rain; and the area of land farmed. A similar review by the University of Hohenheim, Germany, in 2000 reached the same conclusions (Hohenheim is a proponent of organic farming and quoted by the Soil Association).

Myth Two: Organic Farming Is More Sustainable

Organic potatoes use less energy in terms of fertiliser production, but need more fossil fuel for ploughing. A hectare of conventionally farmed land produces 2.5 times more potatoes than an organic one.

Food scares are always good news for the organic food industry.

Heated greenhouse tomatoes in Britain use up to 100 times more energy than those grown in fields in Africa. Organic yield is 75 percent of conventional tomato crops but takes twice the energy—so the climate consequences of home-grown organic tomatoes exceed those of Kenyan imports.

Defra [Department for Environment, Food and Rural Affairs] estimates organic tomato production in the UK releases almost three times the nutrient pollution and uses 25 percent more water per kg of fruit than normal production. However, a kilogram of wheat takes 1,700 joules (J) of energy to produce, against 2,500J for the same amount of conventional wheat, although nutrient pollution is three times higher for organic.

Myth Three: Organic Farming Doesn't Use Pesticides

Food scares are always good news for the organic food industry. The Soil Association and other organic farming trade groups say conventional food must be unhealthy because farmers use pesticides. Actually, organic farmers also use pesticides. The difference is that "organic" pesticides are so dangerous that they have been "grandfathered" with current regulations and do not have to pass stringent modern safety tests.

For example, organic farmers can treat fungal diseases with copper solutions. Unlike modern, biodegradable, pesticides copper stays toxic in the soil for ever. The organic insecticide rotenone (in derris) is highly neurotoxic to humans— exposure can cause Parkinson's disease. But none of these "natural" chemicals is a reason not to buy organic food; nor are the man-made chemicals used in conventional farming.

Myth Four: Pesticide Levels in Conventional Food Are Dangerous

The proponents or organic food—particularly celebrities, such as Gwyneth Paltrow, who have jumped on the organic bandwagon—say there is a "cocktail effect" of pesticides. Some point to an "epidemic of cancer". In fact, there is no epidemic of cancer. When age-standardised, cancer rates are falling dramatically and have been doing so for 50 years.

If there is a "cocktail effect" it would first show up in farmers, but they have among the lowest cancer rates of any group. Carcinogenic effects of pesticides could show up as stomach cancer, but stomach cancer rates have fallen faster than any other. Sixty years ago, all Britain's food was organic; we lived only until our early sixties, malnutrition and food poisoning were rife. Now, modern agriculture (including the careful use of well-tested chemicals) makes food cheap and safe and we live into our eighties.

Myth Five: Organic Food Is Healthier

To quote Hohenheim University: "No clear conclusions about the quality of organic food can be reached using the results of present literature and research results." What research there is does not support the claims made for organic food.

Disease is a major reason why organic animals are only half the weight of conventionally reared animals.

Large studies in Holland, Denmark and Austria found the food-poisoning bacterium Campylobacter in 100 percent of organic chicken flocks but only a third of conventional flocks; equal rates of contamination with Salmonella (despite many organic flocks being vaccinated against it); and 72 percent of organic chickens infected with parasites.

This high level of infection among organic chickens could cross-contaminate non-organic chickens processed on the same production lines. Organic farmers boast that their animals are not routinely treated with antibiotics or (for example) worming medicines. But, as a result, organic animals suffer more diseases. In 2006 an Austrian and Dutch study found that a quarter of organic pigs had pneumonia against 4 percent of conventionally raised pigs; their piglets died twice as often.

Disease is the major reason why organic animals are only half the weight of conventionally reared animals—so organic farming is not necessarily a boon to animal welfare.

Myth Six: Organic Food Contains More Nutrients

The Soil Association points to a few small studies that demonstrate slightly higher concentrations of some nutrients in organic produce—flavonoids in organic tomatoes and omega-3 fatty acids in organic milk, for example.

The easiest way to increase the concentration of nutrients in food is to leave it in an airing cupboard for a few days. Dehydrated foods contain much higher concentrations of carbohydrates and nutrients than whole foods. But, just as in humans, dehydration is often a sign of disease.

The study that found higher flavonoid levels in organic tomatoes revealed them to be the result of stress from lack of nitrogen—the plants stopped making flesh and made defensive chemicals (such as flavonoids) instead.

Despite the "boom" in organics, the amount of land being farmed organically has been decreasing since its height in 2003.

Myth Seven: The Demand for Organic Food Is Booming

Less than 1 percent of the food sold in Britain is organic, but you would never guess it from the media. The Soil Association positions itself as a charity that promotes good farming practices. Modestly, on its website, it claims: ". . . in many ways the Soil Association can claim to be the first organisation to promote and practice sustainable development." But the Soil Association is also, in effect, a trade group—and very successful lobbying organisation.

Every year, news outlets report the Soil Association's annual claim of a big increase in the size of the organic market. For 2006 (the latest available figures) it boasted sales of £1.937bn [billion].

Mintel (a retail consultantcy hired by the Soil Association) estimated only £1.5bn in organic food sales for 2006. The more reliable TNS Worldpanel, (tracking actual purchases) found just £1bn of organics sold—from a total food sector of £104bn. Sixty years ago all our food was organic so demand has actually gone down by 99 percent. Despite the "boom" in organics, the amount of land being farmed organically has been decreasing since its height in 2003. Although the area of land being converted to organic usage is scheduled to rise, more farmers are going back to conventional farming.

The Soil Association invariably claims that anyone who questions the value of organic farming works for chemical manufacturers and agribusiness or is in league with some shady right-wing US free-market lobby group. Which is ironic, considering that a number of British fascists were involved in the founding of the Soil Association and its journal was edited by one of [British politician] Oswald Mosley's blackshirts [Associated with British Union of Fascists] until the late 1960s.

All Britain's food is safer than ever before. In a serious age, we should talk about the future seriously and not use food scares and misinformation as a tactic to increase sales.

4

Non-Organic Foods Are Coated with Pesticides

Vegetarians in Paradise

Vegetarians in Paradise is a Los Angeles–based magazine, distributing vegetarian information to the broader community.

In 2003 the Environmental Working Group identified the "dirty dozen," a list of fruits and vegetables that had the most pesticide residues. The Environmental Working Group found numerous pesticides that were potentially harmful to consumers. Even traces of DDT (dichlorodiphenyltrichloroethane), a pesticide banned in the United States since 1972, were identifiable in certain vegetables. The dangers of pesticides are numerous. Some contain carcinogens, or cancer-causing agents, while others cause birth defects in animals. Although pesticide residue may seem small in an individual serving of fruits or vegetables, eating the five to nine recommended servings of fruits and vegetables each day will lead to greater risk. The best way to avoid pesticide contamination is to switch to organic produce.

You don't want to know what's in the next bite of that juicy peach you're devouring on that hot, summer day. If someone told you that it contained Iprodione, Azinphos methyl, and Phosmet, you might respond with a puzzled look before asking for an explanation. As few of us know, the three chemicals are designed to make sure no other creatures eat that peach before you do. In fact, they are the most common

Vegetarians in Paradise, "Dirty Dozen May End Up on Your Dinner Plate," January 1, 2006. Reprinted with permission.

of 45 different pesticides discovered in laboratory tests on peaches. Those tests revealed that pesticides were present in 94% of peaches examined.

The three pesticides are problematic for both humans and animals. Iprodione is an animal carcinogen [cancer-causing agent]; Azinphos methyl interferes with hormones; Phosmet is a triple threat by being an animal carcinogen, damaging the human reproductive system, and interfering with hormones.

Peaches seem to win the pesticide prize, but 11 other fruits and vegetables are close behind to make up the dirty dozen cited by the Environmental Working Group [EWG]. According to the *EWG Pesticides in Produce* issued in 2003, peaches, apples, bell peppers, celery, cherries, imported grapes, nectarines, pears, potatoes, red raspberries, spinach, and strawberries are the leading pesticide-laden produce items.

Measuring Pesticides in Food

In the *Food News Report Card* the Environmental Working Group ranked 46 common fruits and vegetables for pesticide contamination. Their ranking chart was based on an analysis of over 100,000 tests for pesticides on those foods, conducted from 1992 to 2001 by the US Department of Agriculture [USDA] and the Food and Drug Administration.

The EWG produced a composite score based on six measures:

- Percent of the samples tested with detectable pesticides

- Percent of the samples with two or more pesticides

- Average number of pesticides found on a sample

- Average amount (level in parts per million) of all pesticides found

- Maximum number of pesticides found on a single sample

- Number of pesticides found on the commodity in total

Being at the bottom of the rating scale is not necessarily bad, especially when the scores rank the amount of pesticide contamination. The twelve lowest pesticide purveyors are asparagus, avocados, bananas, broccoli, cauliflower, sweet corn, kiwis, mangos, onions, papayas, pineapples, and sweet peas. Being on this list did not mean the fruits or vegetables were pesticide free, just that they were least likely to have pesticide residues on them.

Eight of the dirty dozen were fruits. Over 90% of nectarines, peaches, and pears tested positive for pesticides, while nectarines, peaches, and cherries were likely to have multiple pesticides on a single sample (over 75%). Peaches and raspberries had the most pesticides on a single sample (9) with strawberries and apples close behind with 8.

Leading the dishonor roll of vegetables were celery, spinach, bell peppers, and potatoes. Celery was most likely to have multiple pesticides and had the highest percentage of samples (94%) test positive for pesticides. It almost edged out spinach for most pesticides in one sample. Spinach counted 10 pesticides with celery registering 9. Bell peppers surpassed both with 39 pesticides, the most overall.

DDT was banned because it caused significant damage to wildlife around the world.

DDT Residues

Although 70% of potatoes were found to have pesticides and its total of 29 pesticides ranked it below celery and spinach, one of those pesticides was DDT [synthetic pesticide, dichlorodiphenyltrichloroethane], which was banned in the United States after December 31, 1972. Samples of spinach also contained DDT.

According to the Natural Resources Defense Council [NRDC], "In soil, DDT lasts for a very long time because it binds strongly to soil particles. Once attached, DDT and its byproducts can persist for as long as 15 years. Moreover, when bound to soil particles, DDT can begin to bioaccumulate, building up in plants and in the fatty tissue of the fish, birds, and animals that eat the plants. Despite a longstanding ban in this country, the United States exported more than 96 tons of DDT in 1991."

The NRDC reported the presence of DDT in breast milk, although there has been a decline in countries that have banned or restricted this chemical. DDT was banned because it caused significant damage to wildlife around the world and was a suspected link to breast and liver cancer. It was also believed to hinder embryo development and reproduction. . . .

Pesticide Dangers

In looking at the test results of the dirty dozen of fruits, one notices that there are other chemical pesticides that have more dangers associated with them. Benomyl and Carbaryl, for example, have five pronounced effects. They are animal carcinogens and cause birth defects in animals. In humans they damage the reproductive system, interfere with hormones, and damage the brain and nervous system. Benomyl and Carbaryl are also found in spinach. Benomyl is also present in peaches and strawberries, while Carbaryl is evident in peaches, strawberries, raspberries, nectarines, imported grapes, cherries, bell peppers, and apples.

Another pesticide heavy hitter is Captan, a carcinogen that causes birth defects in animals. In humans it damages the reproductive system, the brain and nervous system, and the immune system. Captan has found a home in peaches, strawberries, raspberries, pears, imported grapes, and apples.

Since the National Cancer Institute and Produce for Better Health Foundation recommend eating 5 to 9 servings of fruits and vegetables and the Centers for Disease Control and Prevention recommend 5 servings, wouldn't this mean that people would be consuming more pesticides? Not necessarily, if people cut back on eating the items on the dirty dozen list. But that eliminates many vegetables that contribute nutrients beneficial to the human diet.

Going Organic

The best way to scale back pesticide consumption is to go organic. In its annual survey released in 2004, [the Organic Consumers Association] revealed that 68% of Americans have tried organic fruits and beverages compared to 54% in the two previous years. The survey also reported that 27% indicated that they consumed more organic foods and beverages than they did the year before.

The three principal reasons people gave for purchasing organic were avoidance of pesticides (70.3%), freshness, (68.3%), and health and nutrition (67.1%). Avoiding genetically modified foods was the reason given by 55% of the respondents. "Better for my health" was the answer of 52.8% while "better for the environment" was the statement of 52.4%.

The best way to scale back pesticide consumption is to go organic.

The chief obstacle to more purchases of organic items is price with 74.6% of those polled giving that as a reason for not buying more. As a positive sign more Americans (40%) now recognize the organic logo and labeling on their purchases, up 19% from 2003.

Washing Fruits and Vegetables

In response to those who suggest thorough washing of fruits and vegetables to remove pesticides, the Environmental Working Group reminds them that in the tests conducted by the USDA the produce was washed before being analyzed.

"While washing fresh produce may help reduce pesticide residues, it clearly does not eliminate them," says EWG. "Nonetheless, produce should be washed before it is eaten because washing does reduce levels of some pesticides. However, other pesticides are taken up internally in the plant, are in the fruit, and cannot be washed off. Others are formulated to bind to the surface of the crop and do not easily wash off. Peeling reduces exposures, but valuable nutrients often go down the drain with the peel."

In VIP [*Vegetarians in Paradise*] visits to farmers' markets we have noted an increase in the number of farmers selling organic produce during the last seven years. In many cases the fruits and vegetable prices are the same or even less than those in supermarkets. As more and more people purchase and demand organic the prices will come down.

VIP commends the Environmental Working Group for their efforts to make the public aware of pesticides in our food. We agree with their goal of encouraging people to eat a varied diet, wash their fruits and vegetables, and select organic whenever possible.

5

Organic Fertilizers Pose More Health Risks than Pesticides

Stanley Feldman

Stanley Feldman is a medical professional and the author of several text books, including Scientific Foundations of Anesthesia.

Organic food has been promoted as a healthier and tastier alternative to non-organic foods that are reported to be covered with dangerous pesticides. In truth, there is no such thing as non-organic food: all food is made up of organic substances. Whether a farm uses conventional or organic fertilizers, both products provide the same nutrients to soil. Organic fertilizers, however, can contain potentially hazardous bacteria. The use of natural pesticides is likewise misleading: unlike organic pesticides, conventional pesticides are monitored by the government and are completely safe. Despite many inconsistencies and half truths, the organic food market has nonetheless become successful.

*T*HE MYTH: Non-organic foods are covered in harmful pesticides.

THE FACT: One of the pesticides deemed 'safe' by organic producers carries a warning that it is harmful to fish.

As I look back to my childhood, it seems that every summer's day was sunny and filled with joy. I cannot remember it raining so hard that it spoiled a day out in the country. The food tasted better, the tomatoes were juicier, the strawberries tasted sweet and succulent and the peas that came from

Stanley Feldman, "Organic Food," *Panic Nation: Exposing the Lies We're Told About Health and Food.* London: John Blake, 2005, 47–55. Reprinted by permission.

the pods were so delicious that many were eaten raw before my mother could cook them. I realise that my memory is highly selective—there must have been rainy days, rotten tomatoes, sour strawberries and worm-infested peas, but somehow things today never seem quite as good as they were in our youth.

It is the same rose-tinted nostalgia that is used to promote organic food. The cult of natural 'organic food' is based on a belief that, while the sun may not always have shone in days gone by, the food was better and healthier before the advent of modern farming and horticulture, when the crops were liberally fertilised with manure from animal faeces or rotting vegetable waste, in the form of compost.

This belief has been energetically reinforced by the scare stories of the eco-warriors who have blamed every ill—from heart disease and cancer to global warming, pollution, less biodiversity and the rape of the countryside—on the perceived evils of modern farming.

As soon as one spurious claim is disproved another scare is invented. So vociferous and well funded is the propaganda that they have caused many otherwise sensible people, and some government agencies, to embrace the organic bandwagon, although no one has produced any evidence in its favour. By scaring the public, the organic lobby has created a billion-pound market in the UK for food that is up to 40 per cent more expensive than that produced by conventional farming and from which it is indistinguishable.

Organic vs. Nonorganic

The term *organic food* is in itself misleading. The separation into 'organic' and 'nonorganic' was based on the belief that some substances contained a life-giving property: these were originally called 'organic'. In recent times it has come to mean chemicals containing molecules based on a carbon atom. So all food is organic (with the technical exception of water).

There is no such thing as inorganic food. Whenever a pressure group resorts to a nonsense name, in order to suggest that it has nature on its side, that it has the monopoly on what is good, or that it is the only path that faithful followers of purity and truth can take, one should smell a rat.

The Soil Association, the high priests of this cult, believe that chemicals, whether organic or inorganic, are bad, a danger to the consumer, and will possibly bring death to the planet. Natural substances, by contrast, are apparently good. Yet all infections are caused by natural, organic bacteria; many organic substances produced in plants and berries, such as the belladonna of the deadly nightshade and the prussic acid in almonds, are highly poisonous; the 'natural' copper sulphate that is recommended as an organic treatment for fungal infections is so toxic to marine life that copper-based antifouling of boats has been banned in many countries. If a fungicide is not used and the ergot fungus infects cereal crops, then the unsuspecting organic consumer may end up with gangrene of fingers and toes.

In all fairness to the Soil Association, it does permit the use of pesticides provided they come from an approved list. Some have reassuringly innocent names such as 'Soft Soap', which turns out to be octodecanoic acid and carries a label warning that it is dangerous to fish.

Organic Fertiliser

The main thrust of the argument used by adherents of this cult seems to be that organic fertiliser, by which it is implied that it is produced from animal excreta or rotting vegetable waste, is necessary in order to produce food that is both nutritious and safe. This supposition is difficult to support. Manure is teeming with bacteria, many of which are pathogenic, and a few lethal. Compost rots because of the action of these bacteria, and, while they are in the main less harmful than those in manure, most sensible consumers would be reluctant to ingest them in the produce they purchase.

The root systems of plants can absorb only those nutriments that are in solution. They cannot take up particulate matter. Before the plant can use any fertiliser, organic faeces, rotting vegetable waste or chemical additive, it must first be broken down and rendered soluble in water. This necessitates reducing organic matter to its basic chemical form. It is true that in organic fertiliser these are usually more complex chemicals, but they must be rendered into the same simple basic chemicals in the plant before they can be used to encourage its growth.

There is absolutely no rational reason why all the breakdown products of organic fertiliser should not be supplied in a basic chemical form rather than leaving it to the bacteria in the soil to produce them from compost. At the end of the day, the plant uses both chemical and organic fertiliser in the same way in the same chemical processes that are essential for its growth. The main difference is that chemical fertiliser is produced with a standardised value of its content, and does not contain the dangerous bacterial pathogens present in organic waste.

The level of pesticides in our food is carefully monitored and kept below a very conservative safety level.

It was reportedly Prince Albert [husband of British monarch Queen Victoria] who started the vogue for using natural, organic household waste to fertilise the kitchen garden at Osborne House on the Isle of Wight. Prince Albert died of typhoid fever, a disease caused by ingesting food contaminated with the faeces from a carrier who may not have exhibited symptoms of the disease.

Pesticides vs. Natural Compounds

The other canon of organic law is the avoidance of known effective pesticides and the preference for naturally occurring compounds such as sulphur and copper-based chemicals to control infestations. This again is illogical. It is based on the belief that the organophosphate pesticides [those containing phosphorus] are poisonous and naturally occurring chemicals are not. This ignores the fact that sulphur and copper-based ones are also poisonous. Both organophosphate pesticides and naturally occurring chemicals can be poisonous; it is all a matter of dose. The German-Swiss doctor and chemist Paracelsus (1493–1541) pointed out 'nothing is without poison; it is the dose alone that makes it so'. When one looks at those parts of the world where pesticides are not freely available (usually because of cost), it is found that over a third of all the food produced is eaten by pests, whereas in the Western world, where pesticides are used, the loss is reduced by 41 per cent.

The level of pesticides in our food is carefully monitored and kept below a very conservative safety level. The chemicals have a short half-life and have not been shown to accumulate in the body. Their level in food is way below that at which it is likely to cause symptoms, even in the most sensitive individual. Although pesticides in food have been blamed for a variety of ill-defined syndromes, including cancers, extensive medical studies have failed to implicate them as the cause of any known clinical condition. There are no mysterious unknown disease states caused by the prolonged intake of small doses of these chemicals. Since they do not accumulate in the food chain or in the body, chronic toxicity is improbable. As Sir John Krebs, the former chairman of the Food Standards Agency, pointed out in *Nature* in 2002, 'a single cup of coffee contains natural carcinogens equal to at least a year's worth of synthetic carcinogenic residues in the diet'.

The various conditions that have been attributed to these chemicals by the food faddists bear no relationship to any of the known effects of the pesticides. There have been sufficient cases of self-induced organophosphate poisoning to recognise the symptoms of poisoning (pesticides are a common form of suicide in Third World countries). It starts with excessive salivation and lachrymation [tear production] and is invariably followed by painful gut cramps and an uncontrollable twitching of the muscles. Pesticides are not commonly associated with any allergic conditions.

Virtually all the chemical pesticide residue that occurs in food is found on the outside of fruit and vegetables and is easily washed off. If the choice has to be made between pest-infected food, food exposed to bacterial pathogens and minute harmless amounts of pesticide, then to choose not to use them is the equivalent of a patient with pneumonia refusing antibiotics in favour of leeches and bleeding.

There are many mysteries about what constitutes organic food.

Organic Standard

The inconsistent approach of the advocates of organic food becomes apparent when one considers organic eggs. These have to come from organically reared chickens. To be an organically reared chicken, the bird has to eat 80 per cent organic food for six weeks. No effort is made to control the other 20 per cent, which may contain potential carcinogens or toxic material. At the end of that time, any eggs it lays will be deemed organic and therefore much more expensive. Organic eggs and chickens should not be confused with free-range chickens, which can roam more freely and eat whatever they like. Organic chickens are not kept in battery cages. To conform with the organic requirements, they must be allowed 1 square metre of space per 25 lb of chicken.

There are many mysteries about what constitutes organic food. If a banana is squashed and its juice extracted to produce 'banana flavouring', it can be analysed and shown to be the chemical amyl acetate. However, if one produces amyl acetate by adding vinegar to amyl alcohol it cannot be called 'organic'. It is the same chemical, it tastes the same, it smells the same but it is not natural and it is therefore presumed to be bad. The same logic suggests that acetic acid is somehow different from the acid in vinegar, or citric acid from that of lemon-juice extract.

A walk around the organic shelves of a supermarket leaves one amazed at the gullibility of its patrons.

It has been suggested that prepackaged, cleaned lettuce is dangerous, as it is washed in a solution containing chlorine. The initiates of this scare fail to point out that the amount of chlorine residue in the product is less than that found in most swimming-pool water and in some drinking water.

Does Organic Food Taste Better?

A walk around the organic shelves of a supermarket leaves one amazed at the gullibility of its patrons. The produce is not particularly inviting in its appearance, and its taste is, for the most part, identical to that of the normal produce. A ten-year, obsessively controlled trial of foods grown in similar positions, on the Boarded Farm study in Essex [England], compared organically grown crops with those produced by conventional farming, using integrated farm management. The study revealed that the best results, judged by soil quality, effect on bird life, biodiversity and yield, came from the integrated farm management fields. Blind tasting of the crops from these studies failed to reveal any consistent difference between organic and nonorganic produce. This is hardly surprising, since taste is largely a result of the genetic makeup of the particular strain of the crop that was planted, the time it has spent maturing before being picked and the climatic conditions during its growth.

Today, the zealots of the cult of organic food are making ever more irrational inroads into the way we live.

Although most produce, be it organic or not, tastes better when freshly picked, the use of preservatives can prolong the freshness of some produce. Some preservatives are available for use in organic foods but they are seldom used in organic vegetables and fruits, which consequently have a short shelf life—as evidence by wilting lettuces and bendy cucumbers.

The Future of Organic Food

Today, the zealots of the cult of organic food are making ever more irrational inroads into the way we live. They are promoting organic clothing and toiletries with the implied assurance that these are somehow less likely to cause allergies and skin disease. There is no evidence to support this claim, which plays on the fears of parents with children who suffer from skin allergies.

So why do people pay up to 40 per cent more for organic products? Is it a cynical confidence trick to exploit consumer ignorance? Is it the belief that, should little Johnny turn out to have allergies/asthma/autism or a brain tumour, this might have been prevented if he had been brought up on organic food and worn pyjamas made from organic cotton? Or is it simply a matter of choice? It is difficult to believe that the proponents of organic produce are all part of an evil conspiracy to defraud the public, although they often use unworthy, unscientific scare tactics, conjuring up all sorts of disasters to frighten the nonbelievers. Most just seem to be victims of their own propaganda, who yearn after bygone days when the sun shone all the time.

However, there is another side to the story. The food industry has to accept some of the blame. It has too often put cost before quality, marketed fruit picked before it has had time to ripen and mature on the tree, and encouraged the production of food that looks good on the supermarket shelf rather than produce that tastes good when eaten. I believe that our memories of apples picked straight from the tree, tasting crisp and juicy, of strawberries that were sweet and succulent and peas that one could not resist eating raw have some factual basis. It is our desire to get back to the days of real, fresh, ripe fruit and vegetables that has encouraged the spurious market for organic food.

6

The Mass-Marketing of Organic Food Presents an Ethical Dilemma

Katherine Mangu-Ward

Katherine Mangu-Ward is a senior editor for Reason *magazine, and her work has appeared in the* Washington Post, Los Angeles Times, *and the* New York Times.

An original tenet of the organic food movement emphasized the importance of local markets. The mantra, buy local, defined the ethics of many organic food consumers. Over time, however, the buy local tenet would be challenged as larger grocery chains began selling organic food. Many of today's consumers easily accept buying organic food from Wal-Mart and Whole Foods, and express little concern over the need to support local farmers. Organic TV dinners purchased at Wal-Mart may not be what the original organic food movement envisioned, but it is nonetheless a development that consumers are embracing.

Consider, if you will, the dilemma posed by the organic TV dinner.

Such microwavable paradoxes are hardly what ethical eating pioneers of the 1970s envisioned when they founded cooperative farms and tiny dairies. But in the decades since, organic food has become cautiously, steadily more industrialized. More outlets sell organics every day—organic milk is now the fastest growing sector in the beverage market—and grocery

Katherine Mangu-Ward, "Food Fight," *Wall Street Journal*, June 9, 2006. Reprinted with permission.

chains like Whole Foods are expanding so quickly that many suppliers have adopted the techniques of mass production, using trucked-in fertilizer and harvesting machines to keep up with demand.

Still, old-school ethical eaters held onto the notion that, however indirectly, buying pre-washed vacuum-packed organic "baby" carrots shipped from California somehow helped to protect the kind of small traditional farmers who started the movement. But when Wal-Mart announced plans to introduce more than 1,000 new organic products in its stores [in 2006], denial was no longer possible. And that's when the organic compost hit the fan.

Competing for Organic Customers

Michael Pollan, author of *The Omnivore's Dilemma*, calls industrial organic food a "contradiction in terms." Of Wal-Mart's promise to sell organics at a relatively small markup he has written: "To say you can sell organic food for 10 percent more than you sell irresponsibly priced food suggests that you don't really get it."

As the ethical-eating movement falls apart, old allies are fast becoming new enemies. They're competing for customers, market share and legitimacy. Small farmers, their marketers and food gurus have started exhorting ethical eaters to "eat local," "eat seasonal" or to get "beyond organic."

Ground zero for the struggle to decide who owns ethical eating in Manhattan is the shiny new 50,000 square-foot Whole Foods staring across 14th street at the Union Square Greenmarket Farmers Market. The food fight is just starting, with trash talk by both sides recently reported, and it's only a matter of time before the Greenmarket farmers start lobbing locally grown vine-ripened tomatoes and balls of fresh Hudson Valley mozzarella across the street at the new megastore. Hundreds of Whole Foods employees (perhaps with support from nearby Trader Joe's) will retaliate by tossing frozen organic pizzas like ninja death stars and smashing bottles of organic Chilean wine to use the fragments as shivs. Their battle cries will ring out in the early morning air: "Eat Local!" vs. "Eat Organic!"

The Organic Dilemma

How did we get here? Early in the organic movement, participants wanted to opt out of the modern capitalist food supply and try something more, well, groovy. But as the movement grew, more justifications were added. Some eaters got onboard because they were concerned about health—they feared that pesticides, hormones and mercury were taking a toll on our physical well-being. Others liked the idea of supporting family farms and the picturesque landscape they create. Still others decided that food tasted better and fresher when it wasn't part of the culinary-industrial complex.

Early in the organic movement, participants wanted to opt out of the modern capitalist food supply and try something more, well, groovy.

But as justifications for eating ethically proliferated, so did the modes of ethical consumption, creating all sorts of new allegiances, not to mention more chances for sanctimony from certain elitist ethical eaters. For those worried about the effect of chemical pesticides and hormones on their children's development, organic TV dinners are a quick, easy way to do the right thing for their kids. But for consumers who fret about over-reliance on fossil fuels, those same meals—assembled from ingredients grown in a dozen countries, heavily packaged and shipped in freezer trucks—miss the point entirely. Free-range cows don't appease vegetarians concerned about the sustainability of our food supply. And people who campaign for humane treatment of farm animals don't care much about the vast amounts of energy required to import grapes from Chile.

When organics hit the big time, a few movement purists realized factory farms weren't the only enemy. They began to shun industrial organic and its big-store purveyors, instead favoring farmers markets. As a result, these small growers who were initially afraid that Whole Foods would steal their customers are doing a booming business—the number of farmers markets in the U.S. has—more than doubled in the last decade.

Local vs. Organic

Most Americans, of course, remain happily oblivious to the local vs. organic debate. Organics are still a small proportion of overall food sales ($20 billion out of a trillion dollars). But certain celebrities are trying to draw more attention to the issue.

Primatologist Jane Goodall recently published a manifesto called "Harvest for Hope" in which she laments that "we have been hypnotized into believing that it is perfectly reasonable to walk into a supermarket and find any kind of food, from anywhere, anytime of the year." She would prefer us to "think about meals the way our ancestors did," to "preserve the local harvest by freezing fresh fruits and vegetables and leftovers," to "better endure the lean months of winter and early spring."

Organic is now an agricultural method that includes winter blackberries, TV dinners and plastic-wrapped spring greens able to travel 3.000 miles without wilting.

These purists, who apparently think "lean months" build character or something like that, blame Wal-Mart (and Whole Foods and small organic farmers who sold out to big conglomerates) for defining organic down while giving customers a false impression of what organic really means. The happy leaping cow on the label of a gallon of Horizon Organic milk, they say, is no longer representative of the real lives Horizon's cows are leading.

In fact, much of the blame rests with the federal government. When the USDA [United States Department of Agriculture] released revised labeling guidelines for organic foods in 2000, a bare minimum was established. And it turned out that what Uncle Sam wanted farmers to do to earn an organic label (and thus garner a 50% premium, on average, over conventional foods) wasn't all that difficult. Additives like xanthan gum are permissible in processed foods, and many spray-on pesticides with organic precursors are completely kosher. Cows needn't be allowed to wander over photogenic green pastures; dumping organic corn into the feed trough is just as legit. By regulating organics fairly loosely, government stepped into the middle of a contentious moment in the movement's history— and wound up picking winners.

Convenient Organic Food

For better or worse, organic is now an agricultural method that includes winter blackberries, TV dinners and plastic-wrapped spring greens able to travel 3,000 miles without wilting. Advocates of local eating find themselves back on the fringes where they started in the 1970s and speak angrily about industrial organic as "selling out." And perhaps there's truth to that allegation. But as with most sectarian splintering, the opposing sides have more in common than they like to admit.

"We don't think you should have to have a lot of money to feed your family organic foods," Wal-Mart's CEO [chief executive officer] has said. To some, this sounds like a threat— especially to the ethical eating elites who will have to find new ways of distinguishing themselves from the hoi polloi [the masses]—but for most of us it sounds like good news about better food.

7

Large Companies Compromise the Values of the Organic Food Movement

Family Farm Defenders

Family Farm Defenders (FFD) is an organization that supports the small farmer against encroaching agribusiness. Founded in 1994, FFD supports independent family farms and sustainable agriculture. John E. Peck, current executive director of Family Farm Defenders, states that while the information in this viewpoint is relevant, it is also important to know that it is dated, and chain-store practices may have changed.

With large chain stores like Whole Foods, selling organic food is primarily another way to make a profit. While the chief executive officer of Whole Foods, John Mackey, refers to his employees as team members, he has fought worker unionization. He has introduced a variety of specialty organic foods, products that appeal to an upscale market. Ironically, while customers are buying upscale organic foods, the wine, cheese, beer, and bread they fill their carts with may not be that healthy. Even Whole Foods' donations to charities are based on marketing plans designed to bring more customers into the company's stores. Finally, Whole Foods has worked against many local organic markets, preferring to buy organic products from around the world.

Whole Foods is the largest retail giant in the natural food sector in the U.S. with 168 stores nationwide (plus in Canada and Britain) and annual gross sales now exceeding

Family Farm Defenders, "Welcome to Whole Foods: The Walmart of Organic," May 24, 2010. Reprinted with permission.

$4.6 billion. In fact, Whole Foods has grown twice as fast as the leading corporate grocer, Walmart, over the last four years. Started in a humble storefront at the corner of 8th and Rio Grande in Austin, TX back in 1978 by self-described "free market" libertarian and current CEO, John Mackey, Whole Foods grew parasitically throughout the 1990s by absorbing its competitors: Bread & Circus, Fresh Fields, Merchant of Vino, Mrs. Gooch's, Bread of Life, and Wellspring Markets. "If someone had been ruthless enough, or opportunistic enough—or, really, just smart enough—we could've been crushed," Mackey noted in a 2004 interview, "But I don't fear that anymore. We're not that vulnerable anymore. Our culture is too strong. Our locations are too good. And we know so much more than we used to." Today [in 2010], the only contenders left in the ring to challenge Whole Foods are Wild Oats and Trader Joes [sic].

Back in 1992, a year after Whole Foods made its first public stock offering, Mackey proudly declared "we're creating an organization based on love instead of fear." A devote admirer of Star Trek's United Federation of Planets (with a framed poster of the starship Enterprise on his wall), Mackey styles himself a democratic renegade when it comes to corporate management. The Whole Foods' "Declaration of Interdependence" includes such high-minded principles as "satisfying and delighting our customers" and "team-member happiness and excellence."

Most Whole Foods shoppers are kept blissfully ignorant of the labor strife behind the deli counter.

Resisting Unions

Like Walmart's "associates," Whole Foods doesn't have workers—instead they are called "team members." Whole Foods employees are hired on a provisional basis, and after four months co-workers get to decide whether or not someone stays on their "team." Bonuses beyond the base wage rate are pegged according to performance, so just like the televison series "Survivor" a climate of competitive efficiency is internalized. If you're not good enough, it's your "team" that will vote you off the Whole Foods island, not the boss. This type of propaganda and conditioning is supposed to ensure company loyalty.

At the same time, Mackey's personal antipathy towards labor unions and workers rights has become rather notorious within the business world. He once said, "The union is like having herpes. It doesn't kill you, but it's unpleasant and inconvenient and it stops a lot of people from becoming your lover." As early as 1998, Whole Foods refused to endorse the United Farm Workers (UFW)'s campaign on behalf of better conditions and higher wages for California's 20,000 strawberry pickers. In 2000 the U.S. Dept. of Labor even went to court against Whole Foods over $226,000 in overtime wages that had not been paid to obviously disgruntled "team members."

In July 2002, when employees at the Whole Foods in Madison, WI, dared to organize under the auspices of the United Food and Commercial Workers (UFCW), they incurred the wrath of Mackey, who flew into town for a three hour long mandatory "employee presentation." Nonetheless, workers still voted for the union two days later. One of the organizers behind the Madison drive, Debbie Rasmussen, was later terminated for having given a botched latte to a co-worker, Julie Thayer, another union supporter who was also fired. Whole Foods ultimately crushed the fledgling union through persistent NLRB [National Labor Relations Board] challenges (with the help of business union incompetence according to more radical union activists), sending a clear message to "team members" throughout the rest of Mackey's empire....

Most Whole Foods shoppers are kept blissfully ignorant of the labor strife behind the deli counter. According to grocery retail analyst, David Livingston, quoted in the Sept. 15th, 2005 issue of the *Capital Times*, "Whole Foods is so different from conventional grocery stores. They tend to have their own loyal customer base." The apolitical high status nonchalance that pervades Whole Foods can be appealing. To quote Livingston once again, shopping there is sort of "like being part of a cult." Prof. Jerald Jellison of the Univ. of Southern California puts it a slightly different way: "Whole Foods offers a psychological absolution of our excesses. After filling your cart with sinful wine, beer, cheese and breads, you rationalize it's healthy, so that cancels out the negatives."

Whole Foods thinks shopping should be fun.

The "Yuppie" Market

Whole Foods does cater to a largely college educated "yuppie" clientele with incomes of $50,000+, clearly reflected in the pricey vehicles that crowd the parking lot, whether SUVs or hybrids. These so-called "foodies"—people interested in high-quality, gourmet foods and an overall organic lifestyle—are the main customer base for Whole Foods, accounting for about three quarters of all its sales. Indulgence and convenience often go hand in hand, which is why the typical Whole Foods now devotes two-thirds of its shelf space to more lucrative prepared foodstuffs—hence the derisive nickname "Whole Paycheck."

Whole Foods also highly touts its corporate policy of earmarking 5% of net profits towards philanthropy each year. For instance, Whole Foods has been a top rung corporate sponsor of the Food for Thought Festival in Madison, WI. Each Whole Foods outlet can also donate to community non-profit organizations, with an obvious silver lining for company investors. As Mackey explained in an Oct. 2005 "Reason on Line" article: "In addition to the many thousands of small donations each Whole Foods store makes each year, we also hold five 5% Days throughout the year. On those days, we donate 5 percent of a store's total sales to a nonprofit organization. While our stores select worthwhile organizations to support, they also tend to focus on groups that have large membership lists, which are contacted and encouraged to shop our store that day to support the organization. This usually brings hundreds of new or lapsed customers into our stores, many of whom then become regular shoppers. So a 5% Day not only allows us to support worthwhile causes, but is an excellent marketing strategy that has benefited Whole Foods investors immensely."

Hapless organic supporters are now buying Chinese asparagus, New Zealand peas, and Mexican broccoli at their local Whole Foods outlet.

In a March 8, 2005, *USA Today* article, Mackey lamented that "Americans love to eat. And Americans love to shop. But we don't like to shop for food. It's a chore, like doing laundry. Whole Foods thinks shopping should be fun. With this store, we're pioneering a new lifestyle that synthesizes health and pleasure. We don't see a contradiction." While other grocery chains are downsizing, seeking to replicate the feel and appeal of the neighborhood "mom and pop" grocery. Whole Foods is unveiling 80,000 square foot "Super Size Me" behemoths costing $15 million. Within this decadent themepark one can almost imagine Walt Disney and Willy Wonka skipping down the aisles. Lucky visitors will be able to dip a fresh strawberry into a chocolate fountain ($1.59), have junior try on an organic cotton onesie ($14.00), get a 25 minute massage ($50), and even take home a vat of almond butter ($89.99)—all in a hard day's shopping.

Expanding Organic Markets

The new and improved 50,000 square foot Whole Foods superstore now in the works on University Avenue near Segoe Road in Madison, WI, is modeled on a similar big box Whole Foods in Omaha, NE, which boasts an in-house meat smoking station and a wine kiosk where customers can read reviews by [wine critic] Robert Parker simply by scanning the bottle. Other features that Whole Foods is banking will entice in even more well-heeled foodies into the fold include sushi bars, brick oven pizzerias, wi-fi hotspots, walk-in beer coolers, hot donut makers, and gelato stations.

With the skyrocketing popularity of organic—increasing by 20% per year—the organic USDA [United States Department of Agriculture] label no longer means "Grown in the U.S.A." When a Whole Foods outlet opened in Pittsburgh, local organic farmers were told they could not sell to the store direct, but would have to negotiate with a regional warehouse as far away as Maryland. Though no official figures are kept on organic imports, the USDA estimated that over $1.5 billion worth entered the U.S. in 2002. Hapless organic supporters are now buying Chinese asparagus, New Zealand peas, and Mexican broccoli at their local Whole Foods outlet not realizing that their dollars are going elsewhere. Just like Walmart, Whole Foods' interest in the wellbeing of workers and consumers does not translate into respecting their rights, especially when the bottom line comes first.

8

Large Companies Play an Important Role in the Organic Food Movement

Samuel Fromartz

Samuel Fromartz is a business journalist who began his career at Reuters in 1985. His work has appeared in Fortune Business Inc., BusinessWeek, *the* New York Times, *and other publications.*

The Whole Foods grocery chain succeeded by offering a number of organic food products that combined health and taste. This combination of health and taste became part of the organic food trend. Consumers began to define eating organic as healthy, even when they were eating rich, organic chocolate truffles. Whole Foods learned that they could move beyond the standard health food market by offering beer, wine, meat, seafood, and coffee. Whole Foods also focused on making the shopping experience more enjoyable, while continually searching for new products to expand the company's customer base. This included offering a broad range of product lines, including a variety of organic food choices.

Walking though the sliding glass doors into the Whole Foods Market on P Street recently, I perked up upon seeing the bright displays of produce, but noticed that the early romance I felt toward the store had mellowed. I had acquired the slightly jaded mien of the seasoned shopper who

Samuel Fromartz, "Consuming Organic: Why We Buy," *Organic Inc.: Natural Foods and How They Grew.* New York: Harcourt, 2006, pp. 237–45. Reprinted with permission.

could find exactly what he wanted and get out, leaving the more expensive enticements for novices. Since I owned only five shares of Whole Foods stock (I kept them to receive the annual reports), my rationalization that buying whatever I wanted would swell the company's bottom line and thus my own no longer held water. Now more knowledgeable and with a young child, I had become more price conscious and my shopping venues had splintered.

Health food historically meant bug-eaten organic produce, hardy beans and grains, and badly prepared tofu.

My voluminous purchases of Whole Foods's fresh produce slowed between May and October, when I bought at the local farmers' market; in the winter, I shopped for Earthbound organic salad mix at Costco, which priced it about a third less than Whole Foods. I heard about a smaller local supermarket, My Organic Market (MOM's), which stocked a lot of organic goods and had a business model largely premised on undercutting the prices of its bigger rival. ("We don't mark prices up from wholesale, we mark them down from Whole Foods," Scott Nash, MOM's CEO, told me.) Employees also carried your grocery bags to the car—a big plus with a child in tow. Occasionally, I shopped at Trader Joe's, the cheaper, smaller, eclectic food chain. I largely avoided Whole Foods's artisan bread and sprung instead for superior loaves from local bakers and didn't buy much of their high-end cheese, since I discovered a far better artisan shop in nearby Alexandria. But, as Ellen said one day, "We can't shop at a hundred stores!" Whole Foods still ranked as our main supermarket, since it stocked the most of what we wanted in one venue. I also found if I shopped smart and bought its private-label products, I could avoid emptying my wallet. Still, compared with the giddiness I felt a few years back, my loyalty had diminished.

Pleasure and Health

Whole Foods initially hooked me by satisfying two primal impulses articulated by William Grimes in a *New York Times* review of Whole Foods's mammoth supermarket in Columbus Circle [New York City], which opened in 2004. Whole Foods, he wrote, "subscribes to a religion that might be called moralistic hedonism. With an eye to pleasing presentation and attractive packaging, it offers a Venusberg of gustatory temptations, often rarefied, and all guaranteed to be good for you." These two traits—pleasure and health—for too long stood in opposition to one another in the same way that desire clashes with restraint.

Simply presenting organic produce in an attractive setting became a slam dunk against tough, bland supermarket fare.

Health food historically meant bug-eaten organic produce, hardy beans and grains, and badly prepared tofu—their health quotient rising as palatability declined. On the other extreme, gourmands consumed, say, a milk-braised pork loin, butter-whipped potatoes, and yet another plate of chocolate truffles—delicious, but full of cardio-challenging saturated fat and calories. Instead of viewing these camps as opposed and static and choosing one, Whole Foods saw a dialectic and came up with the synthesis; it made healthy food delicious and marketed the perfect meal. Foods with artificial preservatives, colors, flavors, sweeteners, and hydrogenated oils were verboten; so, too, were the agro-industrial brands like Kraft, General Mills, and Coca-Cola. They were replaced with offbeat natural and organic producers like Hain, Eden Foods, Spectrum, and Amy's Kitchen; natural and organic brands like Boca, Cascadian Farm, and Odwalla, owned by the agro-industrial giants; and artisan fare that could run the full gamut of possibilities. Customers could find tofu or a cheeseburger in this world because it was up to them to find the balance, but as retailing consultant Willard Bishop Jr. told me, Whole Foods "did the editing," setting the boundaries of feel-good food.

Whole Foods was hardly alone in this marriage of health and taste, since chefs such as Alice Waters repositioned organic food to emphasize its high quality. Others, like Deborah Madison, showed how spices, fresh herbs, and ethnic techniques could make a vegetarian dish the center of a fabulous meal. The restaurant movement had by the mid-1980s rebelled against stuffy, elite, saucy French fare, coming up with simple dishes made with the freshest ingredients often bought at the farmers' market. Service at the most popular fine-dining restaurants became friendly, rather than haughty, in the same way that Whole Foods's high-end comestibles [food] enticed rather than excluded the customer. At the same time, the organic movement's historic antipathy to artificial and highly processed food dovetailed with a broader perception that "fresh" meant "healthy." The long-winded arguments about soil biology and organic agriculture could never match the visceral appeal of a perfect tomato or peach. Simply presenting organic produce in an attractive setting became a slam dunk against tough, bland supermarket fare, creating the largest segment of the organic marketplace and, not accidentally, the entryway to Whole Foods. A twenty-foot stroll through the pampered produce section convinces the customer of the high quality of organic food and articulates the values of the store, even if only a portion of what it sells is organic.

It should not be surprising that health and nutrition motivate 70 to 80 percent of all organic shoppers, reaching 90 percent among frequent buyers.

Bishop told me Whole Foods's merger of quality goods with a concept of health created a niche in the grocery industry. "One of the reasons they've been so successful is that they are quite clear and consistent about who they are and what they deliver to the customer," he said.

Organic Food and Health

The timing was right because health had become increasingly important to shoppers, even if they had trouble following any consistent regime. Fifty-five percent of Americans cited health as a key motivation in food purchases in 2004 (up from 45 percent in 2000), and 59 percent said they tried to eat healthy food to avoid illness later in life. These consumers weren't looking at food as medicine but as a way to avoid medicine, doctors, and hospitals in the future, just as J. I. Rodale [early advocate of sustainable farming] had in the 1940s. Even among those on a diet (six in ten Americans), the biggest motivation was health (cited by 77 percent). Pesticides, antibiotics, and hormones also played a role in these decisions, since seven in ten Americans report they are "somewhat concerned" about the risk posed by these substances in the food supply. The 28 percent who view them as a "high risk" roughly mirrors the percentage of people who buy organic food regularly.

With this backdrop, it should not be surprising that health and nutrition motivate 70 to 80 percent of all organic shoppers, reaching 90 percent among frequent buyers. Freshness, taste, environmental benefits, and helping small farms are also cited, with those reasons becoming more important as purchases increase.

Organic food persisted and grew precisely because the movement defined organic as a production method rather than a prescriptive diet.

But ordinary consumers wouldn't begin to care about these benefits if organic food remained unpalatable, unavailable, or too closely associated with a fringe diet. Indeed, organic food persisted and grew precisely because the movement defined *organic* as a production method rather than a prescriptive diet such as Atkins, South Beach, the Zone, or Weight Watchers. The benefit came from eating the food, not from avoiding foods or counting calories. In this way, organic food became associated with a "healthy lifestyle," which meant you ultimately decided what made you feel good. Whole Foods's organic chocolate truffles epitomize this for me; they taste good because they contain chocolate, sugar, and saturated fat—not the healthiest mix. Yet by making them organically, Whole Foods tempered the "bad" quotient and transformed them into something "good."

"For years, people said, 'Consumers don't know what organic means,'" said Harvey Hartman, head of the Hartman Group marketing firm, whose clients include Whole Foods. "We knew that. But we also knew that consumers didn't care! They just wanted to feel good that they were doing the right thing."

Expanding the Organic Market

When the cofounder and CEO of Whole Foods, John Mackey, opened the original store, called Safer Way, in Austin, Texas, in 1978, it was a typical counterculture venue that sold only vegetarian fare. But then Mackey and his friends realized if they wanted to grow, they had to loosen their grip on granola and sell meat, seafood, beer, wine, and coffee. "We didn't think they were particularly healthy products, but we were a whole food store, not a 'holy food' store," he told one interviewer.

This brought in consumers of various persuasions beyond the company's core market. Now vegetarians are just one small segment of a wide base that includes health-and-nutrition devotees, fitness fanatics, foodies, environmentalists, and core organic consumers. Since their concerns overlap to a degree, Whole Foods can feed them all, so long as its message remains consistent. Selling meat, for example, might alienate vegans and vegetarians, but Whole Foods is now developing a program to ensure its meat, which is free of antibiotics and hormones, will be raised to "animal-compassionate" standards. While Mackey publicly dismissed the animal-rights activists who initially pressured the company on this issue, he also looked into their arguments, switched from a vegetarian to a vegan diet, and then began a dialogue. He was not about to ban meat in Whole Foods stores, but he decided if animals must be eaten, the ones the company sold would at least be raised humanely. This would further differentiate Whole Foods's meat from the factory-farm fare in conventional supermarkets, and create a common ground for consumers as divergent as vegans and high-protein dieters. The company won the endorsement of People for the Ethical Treatment of Animals (PETA) in 2004, giving the meat, in effect, a vegetarian seal of approval.

As it has grown, Whole Foods has continued to improve the customer's experience.

Making Grocery Shopping Fun

The company's broader success lay in selling this enhanced food in an enticing setting, with a lot of customer coddling—adding another dimension to the idea that healthy food could be pleasurable rather than puritanical. Mackey has said that Whole Foods capitalized on a paradox: Americans loved food and loved shopping, but hated shopping for food. So the stores, in retailing lingo, became "an experience," wowing customers who had long associated grocery shopping with a loathsome taste. As it has grown, Whole Foods has continued to improve the customer's experience. In the late 1990s, when the company gobbled up regional natural-food chains such as Fresh Fields on the East Coast, Mrs. Gooch's Natural Foods Markets in Los Angeles, and Bread & Circus in New England, each of these acquisitions brought much more than real estate; they brought expertise—which was given a chance to flourish in a culture of autonomy.

Mackey allowed each region and store to make decisions and compete so that the best ideas would win. Bonuses reflected a team's performance in the store, so that all had a stake in making the model hum at the ground floor. Mackey envisioned a company that took care of customers first and employees second; then shareholders, the community, and the wider environment. Profit, in short, was the result of a highly competitive and localized customer focus, not the dictates of a control freak at the top.

When I popped into stores in Berkeley, Seattle, Portland, Denver, Boulder, western Massachusetts, New York, and Washington, they looked similar but never alike. Unique offerings at one would later appear at another. Boulder [Colorado] had a stunning Eden-like fresh flower display at the entrance that I soon saw replicated in other stores, even if they did not quite hone theirs to the same effect. Seattle [Washington], a top store, boasted a highly theatrical prepared-foods area all abuzz at dinnertime, with customers mingling as cooks worked an open grill. Whole Foods's store in Columbus Circle took this to the extreme, rolling out Asian, Latino, and Indian food; brick-oven pizza; and sushi. In the mid-Atlantic region, I noticed the company renovated and reconfigured often, expanding meat sections and playing up thick cuts of aged beef once high-protein diets took off. This refinement demanded engagement, which made the stores fun.

Attracting Customers

Whole Foods soared high and dove low to capture more varied customers. Its lower-priced 365 brand of natural and organic food products sold alongside premium artisan fare. This made eminent sense since few brands dominated the organic and natural-food marketplace, leaving it to Whole Foods to, in effect, become a top brand. Reaching high, it slapped an Authentic Food Artisan (AFA) seal on products deemed worthy of discriminating customers. A shopper seeking value might snap up the perfectly acceptable 365 pasta ($0.79) or choose the organic version ($1.29); if less concerned about price, she could reach for the Montebello brand ($2.99), made from wheat grown on the grounds of a former hilltop Italian monastery that has been farmed free of chemicals since 1388, earning the AFA seal. Or, if she sought an even more rarefied plate of spaghetti, she could buy the Rustichella d'Abruzzo offering ($5.29), crafted by a third-generation Italian master using stone-ground, local organic wheat extruded through handmade bronze dies and dried exceedingly slowly. Each product has a slightly different appeal for a particular occasion, such as feeding the kids or impressing a date.

Making Organic Foods Profitable

Mackey has described this work as marrying love and creativity, which might translate to passion and innovation in a more traditional business context. Whole Foods has no employees, only team members; no managers, but team leaders. The company believes the communal character of the tribe gives its workers more than a union ever could, which is why it trumpets a 100 percent union-free shop (a plus on Wall Street). When an organizing drive at its Madison, Wisconsin, store succeeded in 2002, Mackey e-mailed employees that "the temptation to contract into fear and anger is very powerful. Love and forgiveness are the more difficult choices to make." A year later, two organizers said they were unfairly fired and a pro-union Web site claimed Whole Foods played hardball, but the union was out. Perhaps this was tough love, for Mackey's libertarian, New Age vision—as in much of the organic food industry—never included a place for industrial-era unions. In his view, they impeded the team. To dismiss this as corporate greed would be simplistic, however, since the company also limits salaries and bonuses of the highest paid to no more than fourteen times the average and donates 5 percent of after-tax profits to charity, both of which are unusual in corporate America, union shop or not.

If you were an organic or local food purist, vegan fundamentalist, or union agitator, the store might irk you, but for Mackey, losing these customers was the price of success. "What if we only sold organic stuff? We'd . . . cease to exist because not enough of our customers want us to just sell organic," Mackey said in one interview. "They would find it would be too expensive for them; they wouldn't be willing to buy it." To succeed, the business had to connect with an audience beyond the core by offering a wider palate of attributes.

Again, this wasn't unique in the organic food market. Salad mix and soy milk didn't win in the marketplace solely because they carried an organic label, or any other single attribute. The appeal of salad mix derived from the trendy taste of baby greens, the cleanliness of triple washing, the convenient package; for soy milk, it came from the health benefits and improved palatability of soy and a chilled-shelf placement that implied "fresh." As with Whole Foods, an array of overlapping attributes and connotations—along with the ORGANIC label—made these products attractive to a broad customer base. It was the only way to prevail in the marketplace.

9

Organic Food Is Worth the Extra Expense

Alex Johnson

Alex Johnson is an advocate of organic living and writes for Organic Guide.

Many people note that organic food is more expensive than conventional groceries. The reasons are multiple. Organic farming is often more labor intensive, and small organic farms cannot practice economy of scale by spreading costs across a large agricultural output. Organic farms must also follow strict government guidelines to qualify for the National Organic Program. Finally, once organic products have been sold to retailers, the farmer has little control over the price. Although each of these factors increases the cost of organic food, consumers should also calculate the potential health problems caused from eating conventional agricultural products. When one considers the health of one's family, organic food is worth the extra cost.

One of the first questions I'm asked when I let people know that I prefer to consume organic food is, "How can you afford to eat organic food on your salary?" Okay, so I'm the first to admit it, my annual income only places me marginally above the official poverty line. But that isn't to say that I don't have priorities in my life. I have a young family—a wife and two children to be exact. And having spent quite a bit of time in the food processing industry, I know what goes on behind the scenes. And let's just say, I'm not prepared to

Alex Johnson, "Is Organic Food Too Expensive?" *Organic Guide*, September 29, 2007. Reprinted with permission.

accept the routine shortcuts that conventional food processors are forced to take by the large supermarket chains they are subservient to. Call me nuts, but I don't want my daughter growing breasts at seven years old as a direct consequence of the hormones that were routinely pumped into the battery hens whose eggs she ate. And I'm not overly keen for my son to undergo minor surgery at our local hospital only to discover that, due to the rampant overuse of antibiotics in our food chain leading to yet another outbreak of antibiotic resistant staphylococcus aureus [which causes staph infections], they'll have to amputate his leg below the knee in order to save his life. Am I alarmist? No. I'm just a dad with priorities.

Personally, I'd rather spend a few extra dollars to feed my family a small quantity of high quality organic produce. The alternative, as I see it, requires subjecting my family to the constant moving target of what constitutes "acceptable" parameters for human safety. Does that mean I have to stick to a budget? Yes, of course. Does it mean that my wife and I have to be creative in how we shop? Definitely. Okay, so I'm fairly certain that the extra cost associated with organic food is worth it. But why should it cost more you ask? Well, here are the reasons I believe it's reasonable for me to expect to pay a premium for organic food.

Personally, I'd rather spend a few extra dollars to feed my family a small quantity of high quality organic produce.

Labour—one of the downsides of organic production methods is that they tend to be labour intensive. Because there are no pesticides or herbicides used on an organic farm, more people are involved in undertaking routine tasks, such as the removal of weeds in between rows of vegetables. On the face of it, this might not seem like it should add much in the way of additional cost to your box of fruit and vegetables, but if you've ever spent more than a couple of hours in the garden pulling weeds, you've probably got some idea of how time consuming—and therefore expensive—weeding can be.

Scale—organic farms tend to be smaller than conventional farms. I don't think it necessarily has to be this way. In fact, if more consumers switched to consuming organic food, I'm sure we'd see many larger organic farms pop up. But at the moment, your average organic farm tends to be a small-scale operation. The small scale of organic farming operations means that the associated fixed costs and overheads must be distributed across much smaller produce volumes than conventional farms. Unfortunately, this increases the cost to you and me.

Compliance—both organic farms and organic processors must adhere to strict certification guidelines. Apart from the obvious fees associated with achieving and maintaining certification, an enormous amount of staff time, effort and energy is expended in ensuring all necessary specifications are adhered to. These are additional costs that are not incurred by conventional farms or conventional processors.

As consumers, what we need is strong Government that's prepared to stand up to corporate profiteering at the expense of human health.

Retailers—I've spoke directly with some retailers that have told me that organic lines don't move as fast as some conventional lines. For them, this equates to risk and therefore a price premium must be paid by all customers purchasing organic products. And I suspect that some, but by no means all, retailers are riding the wave of organic popularity all the way to the beach at our expense. But the party won't last indefinitely for these retailers. So, shop around.

Conventional lies—I believe that if we were to look at the true economic cost of conventional food, we'd find that the price society as a whole pays for it would be much higher than its shelf price. Pesticides, antibiotics, herbicides, additives, genetic modification—what is the true cost of the health care people require, and will in the future require, as a result of some of these nasties? After all, what is the cost associated with being told that GM [genetically modified] crops do actually cause bowel and colon cancer? Pretty high I would have thought! What was the cost for numerous Britains being told that, as a direct consequence of cows being fed the spinal tissue from other cows to facilitate cost savings, they had developed a rare from of bovine spongiform encephalitis, more commonly known as "Mad Cow Disease". Did the price of the beef mince they picked up from their local supermarket incorporate the real cost to society? No way. But did the artificially low price, and the cynical cost saving use of spinal tissue fed to ruminants, enable a few large corporates to benefit at the expense of both consumers and honest farmers? You're damn right it did!

As consumers, what we need is strong Government that's prepared to stand up to corporate profiteering at the expense of human health. In the interim, we need to make our own choices. So, next time you're agonising over the price of organic food, as I do from time to time, ask yourself what the true price of the conventional alternative really is. Is organic food really worth it? I think so. How about you?

10

Organic Food Is Not Worth the Extra Expense

Andrew Ellison

Andrew Ellison is the personal finance editor of the London Times.

In order to find out whether organic food was worth the extra cost, the Times *conducted an unscientific blind taste test of organic and non-organic food sold at UK grocery chains. While there were significant differences, organic selections were seldom chosen as the tastiest of the choices. Taste my be considered subjective, but the results of the test raised the question: is organic food really worth up to 60 percent more in price if the supposedly superior quality is not obvious? Other claims for organic food—that it is better for the environment or that "nature knows best"—are equally difficult to support. While there may be reasons to buy some types of organic food, overall organic items are not worth the extra price.*

Food marketers and estate agents have much in common. Both use words of inappropriate grandiosity to sell distinctly average products. Where most of us see a shed, estate agents see a Swedish-timber summer outhouse. Where most of us see a burger, food marketers see a grass-fed Highland-reared steak haché.

Usually found on the supermarkets' premium brands, these fanciful descriptions are designed to encourage us to part with

Andrew Ellison, "Organic Food Is a Waste of Money," *Times* (London), September 5, 2009. Reprinted with permission.

a little bit more of our hard-earned cash. But do these supposedly superior products offer anything more than fancy packaging? *Times* Money decided to investigate.

Over the past fortnight, we have been conducting a blind taste test to establish whether it is really worth paying extra for the supermarkets' standard, premium and organic ranges [product lines]. To ensure that we were unbiased, we chose foods that were hard to tell apart by appearance alone, such as chicken breasts, apples, broccoli, tea, white wine and yoghurt. The results are surprising, but perhaps not for the reasons that you might expect.

The idea that organic food is worth more because it is healthier is totally bogus.

Blind Taste Test

For a start, the difference in taste between the supermarkets' cheapest ranges was huge. Overall, Waitrose's Essentials range was judged to be by far the tastiest of all the ranges at all of the supermarkets. The Sainsbury's Basics range, however, was judged to be by far the worst of all. But the most revealing result is how badly organic food performed.

The organic brands at Tesco, Waitrose and Asda scored worse than each supermarket's basic, standard and premium ranges. Only at Sainsbury's did organic food not come bottom, and that was only because its Basics range is so bad. Hard though it may be to believe, Asda's standard range scored higher than Waitrose's organic range.

Remember, this was a completely blind test—we had no idea what we were tasting, we simply gave each food a mark out of ten based on how much we liked it. Of course, taste is purely subjective and our experiment did not have the scale or scientific rigour to be conclusive. Nonetheless, the results are fascinating and suggest that it is not worth paying extra for organic food. (Which? [a product testing website] estimates that organic food costs on average 60 per cent more than conventional produce).

Inevitably, the organic lobby will dismiss our findings. The Soil Association, which relies on brand organic for its livelihood, defends the industry with a passion that borders on blind faith. But the arguments that it uses are spurious at best.

Is Organic Food Better?

The idea that organic food is worth more because it is healthier is totally bogus. Only last month the Food Standards Agency, the unbiased government agency set up to protect the public's health, published a report concluding that organic food has no greater nutritional value than conventional produce.

The idea that organic food is better for the environment is also questionable. Organic milk, for example, generates more carbon dioxide emissions than standard milk and uses significantly more land.

Then there is the pesticide question. High doses can indeed cause cancer and birth defects. However, there is no evidence that the miniscule amounts found in conventional food are harmful. In fact, some studies have shown that the incidence of cancer among farmers, who are routinely exposed to relatively high levels of pesticide, is lower than in the wider population. In the past 50 years, since synthetic chemicals have come into wide use, average life expectancy has increased by more than seven years.

The origins of the myth that organic is somehow better are complex—in part a result of recent food scares that have made consumers suspicious of modern farming methods, and in part a result of tireless campaigning by pressure groups that exploit the media's desire for sensationalist headlines.

Organic Does Not Equal Quality

Support for organic farming seems based on the belief that "nature knows best". Sadly, this is little more than nostalgia for a golden age of small-scale and simple farming that never really existed. Before intensive agriculture, pesticides and artificial fertilisers, food supplies were constantly endangered by drought and disease. Agriculture was associated with grinding poverty, intensive labour and low yield.

Of course, this is not to say that all organic food should be avoided. The animal welfare standards of organic farmers are generally considered better than average. And as our test demonstrates, some organic foods, such as burgers, do seem to taste better. But consumers should be aware that with organic food in general, they are not paying a premium for real quality, just the perception of such.

11

Government Subsidies Could Lower the Cost of Organic Food

Christy Harrison

Christy Harrison has worked as a senior editor at the green life-style magazine, Plenty *and wrote for* Gourmet.

While organic food has become more popular, increased sales have not led to lower prices. Partly this is related to common organic farming practices: many organic farms are small. Unlike large commercial farms, many fruits and vegetables must be harvested by hand, leading to higher labor costs. Another factor centers on government financial assistance, in the form of subsidies: conventional crops are subsidized in the United States, while organic crops are not subsidized. In order for organic foods to reach more consumers, there must be a stable market for organic products. This could potentially be achieved by providing consumers with better information about organic food—in essence, educating shoppers on the benefits of organic products.

A recent study [in 2010] by researchers at the University of California [UC]-Davis reported that U.S. shoppers who consistently choose healthy foods spend nearly 20 percent more on groceries. The study also said the higher price of these healthier choices can consume 35 to 40 percent of a low-income family's grocery budget. That's bad news for public health. It's also bad news for the organic-food market, since organics usually carry the highest price tag of all the healthy stuff out there.

Christy Harrison, "The (Still) High Cost of Organic Food," *Earth Easy*, May 2010. Reprinted with permission.

Eventually, analysts keep telling us, demand for organics will set the wheels in motion that will drive prices down. But eventually never seems to come. Even though organics sales are growing by about 20 percent a year—almost 10 times the rate of increase in total U.S. food sales, according to the *Nutrition Business Journal*—these cleaner, greener products still carry a hefty premium.

How many shoppers have to jump on the organic bandwagon before we actually see prices fall? How long will that take? And what's the government's role in all this? It depends who you ask.

Today, roughly three-quarters of conventional grocery stores carry natural and/or organic food.

Be Fruitful and Multiply

The organic market we know today began evolving in the 1960s and '70s, when rising environmental awareness led to a backlash against pesticides and increased demand for "green" products. Over the last 20 years, the market has flourished, gaining enough stature to merit the introduction of nationwide U.S. Department of Agriculture [USDA] certification standards in 2002. (Those guidelines have been attacked by some for being too weak; some producers also cause confusion by claiming to be "natural" or "sustainable" without being certified.)

Today, roughly three-quarters of conventional grocery stores carry natural and/or organic food, according to a 2002 Food Marketing Institute study. Restaurants across the country, from the high end to the greasy spoon, are plunking organic ingredients onto their menus. Still, organics represent only about 2 percent of the food industry, both in the U.S. and worldwide. And less than 10 percent of U.S. consumers buy organic items regularly, according to survey data from

Nutrition Business Journal and the Hartman Group, a research firm specializing in the natural-products market. The $10.8 billion industry may be booming, but it's not even close to overtaking conventional sales.

This is in part because of plain old economics. According to basic economic principles, in the short term, as demand grows, prices climb along with it; this small supply and growing demand is what's now getting us, say, $4 quarts of milk. But in the long term, if the market continues to expand, consumption of organics should reach a higher plane where the cost per unit of processing, marketing, and distributing products is much lower. In other words, organic producers will build economies of scale. That price break, in turn, "could bring many more consumers into the market," says Thomas Dobbs, a sustainable-agriculture economist at South Dakota State University. Trouble is, no one seems to know for sure when that will happen.

That's because there are still so many exceptions to the rules, says Steven Blank, an agricultural economist at UC-Davis. Most organic farms in the U.S., for instance, are still small, often family-run operations that don't necessarily fit the economy-of-scale model, because they don't usually have high distribution costs that could be cut as demand rises. Many rely on farmers' markets, community-supported agriculture, and other small-scale distribution channels. "We're too local and hands-on for high distribution to change our costs significantly," confirms Sarah Coddington, co-owner of Frog Hollow Farms in northern California.

Small Farms, Intense Labor

And when the little guys grow delicate crops like peaches and plums that have to be handpicked, Blank says, they can't reach the same economies of scale as farmers who harvest mechanically—their labor costs are too high. "If we have a bumper crop [an unusually large harvest], everything costs more to do," says Coddington.

Frog Hollow's tree-ripened fruits have developed a nation-wide reputation, and a single, succulent peach can run more than $3. But generally, "it" fruits from small farms are not the ones causing a strain on the bank account. Most organic fruits and vegetables—the largest sector of the organics market—are only 10 to 30 percent more expensive than their convention-ally grown counterparts, and Dobbs says many people are willing to pay that kind of markup for better produce. Where economies of scale could really make a difference is in the world of frozen produce, processed foods, and animal prod-ucts.

Those items typically cost 50 to more than 100 percent more than their conventional counterparts, according to a 2002 USDA study. In a survey conducted by Colorado-based Walnut Acres—which bills itself as America's first organic-food company—price was a major barrier for nearly 70 per-cent of shoppers who didn't usually buy organic items.

So to win these folks over, do organic producers have to start offering cheap cheese and budget bonbons? Dobbs makes a surprising estimate: if just one-third of American shoppers bought organic foods on a regular basis, most prices would come down to that 10 to 30 percent markup we're seeing on produce today.

Still seems expensive, but Dobbs says a third of U.S. con-sumers could afford to buy at today's prices if we chose to. The reason we can afford more than we think? We're already paying that much—and more—for supposedly cheap food.

More than Meats the Eye

Conventional crops are heavily subsidized by the federal gov-ernment in the United States, making them artificially inex-pensive. Couple those subsidies—which have been in place since the New Deal [a domestic reform program from the 1930s]—with the cost of cleaning up pollution and treating health problems created by conventional farming, and we're paying a lot in taxes in order to pay a pittance at the grocery store.

"When we make the argument that low-income people can't afford organics, we're assuming that the prices of conventionals are the prices we should be paying," says a USDA economic researcher who asked to remain anonymous. "But those prices externalize a lot of costs, like pollution and higher energy inputs."

A study last year by Iowa State University economists showed that the annual external costs of U.S. agriculture—accounting for impacts such as erosion, water pollution, and damage to wildlife—fall between $5 billion and $16 billion. . . . And Michael Duffy, a coauthor of the Iowa paper, says his team's estimate is conservative.

Subsidizing Organic Farms

So will this drive frustrated consumers to the o-side? Hardly. If anything, the taxes consumers already pay to support conventional farming are a disincentive to paying "double" for organics. To encourage a shopping shift, as European agricultural researchers Stephan Dabbert, Anna Maria Haring, and Raffaele Zanoli write in *Organic Farming*, government has to throw farmers a bone.

"In Western Europe, most countries have decided that organic agriculture needs special support to bring production [and consumption] up to a significantly higher level," Dobbs notes. In countries including Denmark, Sweden, Germany, Austria, and Switzerland, and also at the European Union [E.U.] level, governments contribute to organic markets. In fact, many European policy makers treat organic farming as an instrument to help mitigate environmental problems, manage marginal lands, and address falling farmer incomes, according to Dabbert, et al.

Meanwhile, in the U.S., scant federal money is set aside strictly for organic farmers. The industry doesn't even have access to the type of pricing data and guarantees available to conventional farmers, says University of Georgia agricultural economist Luanne Lohr. "In order to induce producers to get into the [organics] market, they need to know what kind of prices and revenue they're looking at," she says. Without that information, "the producers are flying blind," at the mercy of large distributors who can set unfair prices. "A lot of people would be willing to go into organic, but they don't want to just throw away their investment [in their conventional farms] to get into a system in which they don't have price guarantees," says Lohr.

The success of the USDA's Natural Resources Conservation Service, which dispenses grants that help conventional farmers implement more sustainable practices, suggests subsidies are a key part of encouraging such changes. Deputy Chief Tom Christensen reports that so many farmers are interested in the $3.9 billion program that only one in four applicants is given funding.

In the U.S., scant federal money is set aside strictly for organic farmers.

Loaves and Wishes

Subsidies are a useful way to increase supplies, experts say, but they're only effective in conjunction with a well-run market. "Regulations that promote organic agriculture by encouraging supply are not . . . sufficient to ensure the continuous growth of the organic sector," wrote Nadia Scialabba, a senior officer of environment and sustainable development for the U.N. [United Nations], in 2001.

Scialabba cited the case of Austria, which was the leading organic producer in the E.U. in the mid-1990s. About 10 percent of farmers in the country decided to go organic because of subsidies offered by the government, but this increase in supply was met with inadequate information, distribution, and marketing channels; as a result, many threw in the trowel. They had the money—they just needed a market.

Some other policies that would effectively increase supply have been contentious. For instance, the USDA has been criticized for allowing dairy farmers to be certified while still in the process of converting conventional cows to organic status. (Such status depends on the grain fed to the cows.) Somewhat ironically, a ruling this January that reversed that provision could hurt the market, at least temporarily. Some of the companies making "organic" products under the weaker standards might jump ship due to the higher production costs under the stricter guidelines, says Lohr. This could slow progress "as the industry reorients itself" around the new rules, she says.

The Future of Organic Markets

Such dilutions and confusion can cause consumers to lose trust in the organic label and stop buying, according to a 2002 report presented by German researchers to the U.N. Environment Program. Lohr predicts that the rules will continue to be challenged in years to come, "because if there's demand for organic, people want to make it easy for farmers to become certified."

One thing is clear: though organics have been around for a half-century, unknowns still rule. Long-range studies are few and far between, says UC-Davis' Blank. And most economists don't wager a guess on when pricing will change. For now, in the absence of federal support, they put their money on consumer education driving the market.

"It's a matter of the public really knowing what they get when they buy organic," Blank says. The necessary increase in demand, he adds, is likely to happen only if shoppers develop a pro-organic philosophy before they ever set foot in the store.

12

The Organic Food Market Faces Many Challenges

Kimberley Kindy

Kimberley Kindy writes for the Washington Post; *Kathleen Merrigan serves as the Deputy Secretary for the United States Department of Agriculture (USDA).*

In an interview with Kimberly Kindy of the Washington Post, *the deputy secretary of the USDA, Kathleen Merrigan, discusses the challenges that the National Organic Program and the organic food market are facing. First, Merrigan notes, the rules instituted by the USDA in relation to the National Organic Program are adequate, but need to be consistently enforced. Active enforcement would assure consumers of the quality of the organic food they purchase. Secondly, Merrigan believes that consumers need to be convinced that organic food does not have to be expensive. By active enforcement and consumer education, markets for organic products will continue to grow.*

Kathleen Merrigan, deputy secretary at the Agriculture Department, sat down with *The Washington Post* to discuss the agency's eight-year-old National Organics Program and the challenges ahead for the organics market, which is growing as much as 20 percent a year. In an investigation published last year, *The Post* pointed to several problems in the program, including the agency's failure to discipline violators and to properly test products labeled organic. The USDA's

Kimberley Kindy, "USDA's Deputy Secretary Discusses Challenges for the Organic Food Market," *Washington Post*, April 6, 2010. Reprinted with permission.

[United States Department of Agriculture] inspector general [IG] issued a report last month identifying the same problems and calling for changes.

Kimberly Kindy: *What is the greatest challenge you face implementing reforms recommended by the inspector general so consumers know they are getting high-quality organic products?*

Kathleen Merrigan: I like to call this the age of enforcement.... There is always that period of time when people are adjusting to a new rule. What are the laws of the land? How do I comply? It is 2010. There is no longer any question about what the rules are, and there is no longer any forgiveness of any significant amount in the system for lax enforcement, for failure to comply. Among the things that the inspector general report pointed out was that we need to upgrade our enforcement mechanisms, and we are very much doing so.

Organic foods can be found at farmers' markets, Wal-Mart and grocery stores like Safeway.

How much time do you think it will take?

We have already begun. We are already in the process of putting residue-testing expectations at a higher level ... so part of this is just getting our [organic] certifying agents that we accredit to do the job that they are supposed to do. We don't have to do big rulemaking. We don't have to get huge new budgets. We don't have to come up with huge new visions. We just need to do the job that was set forth in the law.

You helped develop the USDA's organic labeling rules in 1999–2001, but the program was largely shaped and implemented after you left. When you returned to the USDA last year, what was the most surprising thing you learned about what had happened with the program?

I left a pretty long to-do list when we published the final rule. Case in point: pasture.... What does it mean when we say "access to pasture," for ruminants, particularly dairy cows? . . . Well, that was on the list when I left in 2001. . . . There were a lot of things on that to-do list. I inherited that list right back.

The problems with the organics program cited in the IG report took place during the [George W.] Bush administration. What happened? Was it a lack of will? A lack of resources? Were they too friendly to big organic producers?

I assume it was not a priority.

What do you think is the biggest misconception that Americans have about organic products?

That organic has to be super expensive. I don't think it has to be, and with the growth in the industry we are seeing, some of those prices have come down. I think a lot of people think it is the white-tablecloth yuppies, the foodies who buy organic. . . . But organic foods can be found at farmers' markets, Wal-Mart and grocery stores like Safeway.

If consumers are choosing to use their food dollar to support that environmental system [purchasing junk food], I think that's fine.

What would you recommend to consumers who want to find pesticide-free, organic products they can count on?

First, I'd tell them that organic is no guarantee that it is pesticide free. Organic farmers are allowed to use certain pesticides, and sometimes they are natural. I think one thing they can do is go to the [USDA's] Ag Marketing Service's pesticide-testing program (http://www.ams.usda.gov/pdp). We do supermarket sampling all over the country. We go into supermarkets just like Mom or Dad would do and we buy different produce, different foods, dairy, and we test them for pesticide residue. We put all our results on that Web site.

Do you buy organic products? What kind?

I do, but not exclusively. My husband does most of the grocery shopping. . . . We are more inclined to spend money on organic on the perimeters of the grocery store. So we are spending most of our time in the produce, meat, dairy aisles and not so much in the middle, where the processed foods are.

A small percentage of synthetic ingredients is allowed in products like organic cake doughnuts, marshmallows and macaroni and cheese. Should the USDA grant exemptions like this to find an organic path for junk and comfort foods?

I think yes. Obviously, I think so because it was in the law and in the final rule. Again, for me, organic has a very strong environmental connection, and people are always going to eat a certain amount of junk food, and if that junk food arrives in the supermarket and it has come from the most environmental, sound production regimes possible, I think that's great. So if consumers are choosing to use their food dollar to support that environmental system, I think that is fine. So you will sometimes see organic junk food in my basket as well.

As you look ahead, what important developments do you see for organic foods and the program?

I think consumers sometimes feel conflicted. Do I buy organic or do I buy local? . . . We are trying to find ways to grow domestic food markets to help rural communities. . . . And I think the extent to which we can expose [to the public] that overlap between organic and local/regional [producers] will help. I think there are some opportunities there that haven't been explored.

13

Organic Farming Offers Learning Opportunities for Volunteer Workers

Tracie Cone

Tracie Cone is an award-winning journalist and has won a Pulitzer Prize for her writing while working at the Miami Herald.

In recent years, hundreds of people have become organic farm hands through the organization World Wide Opportunities on Organic Farms USA. Known as woofers, these workers are assigned to organic farms around the world where they work for room and board. The program has allowed people to experience both rural living and a variety of ethnic cultures. While every woofing experience does not turn out perfectly, the program has offered hundreds of people the chance to travel and learn more about organic food production.

The morning sun lights up blue lupin and magenta owl's clover as Erik Ramfjord and Andrew Riddle scoop soured milk into a trough, drawing delighted squeals from a dozen free-range pigs.

A month ago [in March 2010], Ramfjord was an unmotivated biology major in Oregon, and Riddle didn't know what he wanted from Humboldt State University in northern California. Now they are energized, toiling from sun up to sun down for meals and a bunk on an organic ranch in central California, hundreds of miles from home.

Tracie Cone, "Organic Farm Volunteers: The New Beat Generation?" *Salon*, April 30, 2010. Reprinted with permission.

"I consider myself extremely lucky to have stumbled upon this," says Ramfjord, 20.

Ramfjord and Riddle each paid $20 to become part of World Wide Opportunities on Organic Farms USA, a group with 9,000 members known by a variation of its acronym, woofers. It's kind of a new millennium version of the traveling hobo willing to work for a meal.

The website allows willing workers to negotiate a non-paid work stint with nearly 1,200 U.S. farmers and ranchers. Every farm could use an extra hand, but the hosts also benefit from the parade of characters who become a part of their lives, if only temporarily.

Most [woofers] are young people from urban areas who want to experience rural life.

Experiencing Rural Life

"When I was younger, I used to hitchhike; it's not the same, but it is that idea," said Ryan "Leo" Goldsmith, executive director of WWOOF-USA, founded with former classmates at the University of California, Santa Cruz. "You have to have faith in humanity and that showing up at someone's house is going to be OK. The tie that binds is a shared interest in sustainable agriculture."

Most are young people from urban areas who want to experience rural life. Some are newly jobless, or don't have prospects. Membership has skyrocketed as the economy has plummeted, soaring from about 1,600 willing U.S. workers in 2005. More than a dozen other autonomous branches match workers with farmers around the globe.

After a year woofing across the U.S. with her boyfriend, Jennifer Makens of suburban Detroit plans to ditch her teaching career to farm for a living. But first the couple will woof on a farm in Pennsylvania, then California and Oregon, Costa Rica, Ecuador, Argentina, Japan and New Zealand.

"I had no idea we'd do this for so long," said Makens, 29, who travels with Charlie Ryan in a Saturn with 150,000 miles on it. "We're getting proud of all the calluses on our hands. It has really changed the way I feel about material possessions, as well. If it won't fit in my car, I don't need it."

Ramfjord heard about woofing while a student at Lewis and Clark College in Portland [Oregon], so he signed up while awaiting a guide job on the American River in California. Riddle will work this summer with the California Conservation Corps.

Making Worldwide Connections

On the Douglas Ranch, about 75 miles south of San Jose [California], they start their day with the pigs, move to milking Bonnie the cow and feeding horses and lambs, then take on whatever owners Don and Rani Douglas need done. It ends at sunset with the cow's second milking and another round of feeding.

The Douglases have hosted woofers since 2005. They've made connections with people from Italy, France, Belgium, South Korea, Scotland and England, and across the United States. Forty in all.

"Besides all the hard work that they do for us, it's been a wonderful experience meeting them all," Rani said.

At South Carolina's Utterly Awesome Goat Farm, the owners need someone to tend Nubians and build a barn addition. West Elk Ranch in Colorado wants help with a garden and vineyard.

Having woofers at Butternut Farms has allowed Patricia West-Volland to hang onto the 20-acre farm in Glenford, Ohio, since the death of her husband a year ago.

"I truly could not stay on this farm without their help," she said.

Not all experiences are good, so Goldsmith encourages woofers to make sure expectations are clear, including how long the visit will last. One left a Georgia farm when an emotionally unstable neighbor joined the crew. One host said a worker broke candlesticks when she asked him to leave.

But usually it works out.

Understanding Food Production

"The first night I was sketching out," Ramfjord said. "I was with people I never met. I thought, 'I'm a dead man.'"

One day an outbuilding needs a new roof, or Ike the pet buffalo has broken a fence, or the cow's eye infection needs medication. They talk excitedly about what they have learned.

"Oh, man, how to drive a tractor, how to use a chain saw, how to roof a house," Ramfjord began.

"How to milk a cow, how to brand, how to dehorn a cow," Riddle continued.

"How to fix a barbed wire fence," Ramfjord added.

"I've extracted a dead pig from Vicki, which was different," Riddle said, and they stop briefly because Vicki did not survive and left two orphans, a harsh reality of ranch life.

"Just being around a pig," Ramfjord offered, then adds: "How you can use a tractor for anything."

Both said they have a better understanding about the labor that goes into food production, and a new awareness about its origins.

"I definitely want to eat meat from a place like this, not a factory farm," Ramfjord said, then he paused and surveyed the green hills around him. "I consider myself extremely lucky to have stumbled onto this ranch."

14

Organic Farm Workers Are as Mistreated as Non-Organic Farm Workers

Jason Mark

Jason Mark co-manages San Francisco's Alemany Farm. He is the coauthor, with Kevin Danaher, of Insurrection: Citizen Challenges to Corporate Power.

Workers on organic farms are frequently treated as badly as workers on conventional farms. While consumers of organic food often assume that the United States Department of Agriculture (USDA) oversees labor, the organic label issued by the USDA only addresses food growth and production, not labor practices. Although the organic food market is growing, the growth has not aided the farm worker. Instead, organic market growth has encouraged corporate companies to enter the organic market, and these corporations have focused on profits, not wages. One solution to the farm labor problem is to create a "fair made" label for food in the same way that these labels are used to identify fair made products imported from other countries. A fair made label, however, would require time to put into practice. In the interim, organic farm workers will continue to work under difficult conditions.

When Elena Ortiz found a job on an organic raspberry farm after working for nine years in conventionally farmed fields, she was glad for the change. The best part about

Jason Mark, "Workers on Organic Farms Are Treated as Poorly as Their Conventional Counterparts," *Grist*, August 2, 2006. Reprinted with permission.

her new job was that she no longer had to work just feet away from tractors spraying chemical herbicides and pesticides. An added bonus was the fruit itself—"prettier," she said, and firmer, which made it easier to pick.

But when it came to how Ortiz was treated by her employers, little was different. Her pay remained meager: $500 a week at peak berry-picking season, but as little as $200 a week during much of the year, leaving her and her farmworker husband with little money to buy fruits and vegetables for their five children. The supervisors at her farm, Reiter Berry, were often "aggressive" and capricious. Rules were arbitrary; workers were sometimes closely monitored, but sometimes allowed to work independently. They were, said Ortiz, assigned to "better or worse rows"—all depending on the whims of the supervisors.

When organizers from the United Farm Workers [UFW] encouraged the Reiter employees to form a union, the company allegedly responded with intimidation and harassment.

"There was an atmosphere of fear. People were afraid they would be laid off," Ortiz said in a recent interview. (Elena Ortiz is not her real name; fearful of losing her job, she spoke only on condition of anonymity.) "I wish they would treat us better. What can the people do? Nothing."

Garland Reiter, one of the co-owners of the company, took objection to Ortiz's comments. "I think we're a leader in the industry, living by honesty, openness, and respect," he said.

While the [organic] seal covers a range of environmental practices, it says nothing about labor conditions.

Organic Farms and Conventional Wisdom

Nevertheless, it appears that worker abuse in the organic industry is widespread.

"There's a common conventional wisdom by a lot of consumers, especially at the higher-end stores, that just because it's organic the workers are treated better," said UFW spokesperson Mark Grossman. "And that's simply not true."

That disconnect between reality and public perception is of increasing concern to farmworker advocates, food activists, and some farmers, who worry that as the organic sector replicates the abusive conditions of conventional agriculture, it is sacrificing the founding values of the sustainable-food movement. The desire to return organic to its roots is driving a slew of initiatives to develop labor standards for organic farms. If successful, the new standards would establish the organic sector as the kind of fully sustainable industry—both socially responsible and environmentally sound—that could be a model for the entire economy.

Where Have All the Hippies Gone?

When you go to the supermarket and buy produce or packaged goods that carry the organic label, you can feel confident that the food was grown under rigorous environmental standards. The U.S. Department of Agriculture's [USDA] organic seal, which debuted in 2002, is a guarantee that your fruits and vegetables were cultivated without petroleum-based fertilizers or (with rare exceptions) synthetic chemicals, and that they aren't genetically modified. The organic label, however, goes only so far. While the seal covers a range of environmental practices, it says nothing about labor conditions.

Although comprehensive studies of conditions on organic farms are hard to find, complaints like Ortiz's are not uncommon. For example, Willamette River Organics, one of Oregon's largest organic operations, has been hit with several lawsuits charging violations of minimum-wage laws. A Human Rights Watch report on the exploitation of adolescent workers said the atmosphere at Arizona's organic Pavich Farms was "hostile, suspicious," with laborers apparently not permitted to speak to inspectors. Threemile Canyon, a large organic dairy and potato farm in Oregon, faces accusations of sexual discrimination in its hiring practices.

Workers get no consolation in the form of higher wages or better benefits, either. According to a report published last year by researchers at UC [University of California]-Davis, a majority of 188 California organic farms surveyed do not pay a living wage or provide medical or retirement plans. In fact, most organic workers earn the same as those in conventional fields—less (adjusted for inflation) than they were making in the 1970s, when the famous UFW boycotts occurred. "The exploitative conditions that farmworkers face in the U.S. are abysmal—it's a human-rights crisis," said Richard Mandelbaum, policy analyst at the Farmworker Support Committee. "In terms of wages and labor rights, there's really no difference between organic and conventional."

While organic's profitability would suggest that there is plenty of money to pay workers better, much of the profits go to retailers and wholesalers higher up the food chain.

If that doesn't seem to fit the organic movement's hippie and homesteader origins, the incursion of big business may be partly to blame. Reiter Affiliated Companies, where Ortiz works, is a perfect example of how the movement has shifted. With thousands of employees, Reiter is the biggest supplier to Driscoll Berry, one of the country's largest distributors of strawberries, raspberries, and blueberries. Driscoll sells both conventionally grown and organic berries—an indicator of organic's growing popularity, but also a sign of how some companies see organic more as a market niche than as a broad business philosophy.

Corporate Organic Farming

That niche is now a $14 billion industry in the U.S. Giant food-processing corporations, seeing opportunities for expansion, have become major players in the organic industry. For example, General Mills owns the organic brands Cascadian Farm and Muir Glen. Kellogg owns Sunrise Organic. Even agribusiness giant ConAgra is in on the act, recently introducing organic versions of its Orville Redenbacher popcorn and Hunt's tomato sauce brands.

And while organic's profitability would suggest that there is plenty of money to pay workers better—for those so inclined—much of the profits go to retailers and wholesalers higher up the food chain. Raising workers' wages is also complicated by the fact that organic labor costs are disproportionately high, since such operations often depend on hand weeding in place of chemical herbicides.

[One] obstacle toward improving conditions is that, simply put, the treatment of farm laborers doesn't rate high on most people's list of concerns.

Ultimately, paying workers more depends on paying farmers more, which appears unlikely in a country that has gotten used to cheap food. "People look down on farmers," said Tim Vos, one of the co-owners of California's Blue Heron Farm, which pays its 10 field workers about $12 an hour. "If you want to pay people well, you need high prices. What would it take to offer benefits? We would have to almost double our prices."

Workers' Rights

Another obstacle toward improving conditions is that, simply put, the treatment of farm laborers doesn't rate high on most people's list of concerns. At least, that's the conclusion of a recent consumer study conducted by researcher Phil Howard at UC-Santa Cruz. The survey found that workers' rights ranked fifth on a list of food-related issues that interested respondents—right behind the treatment of animals.

Farmer Jim Cochran put it bluntly: "Everybody cares about how the bugs are treated, but nobody cares about how the workers are treated."

Cochran knows what he's talking about. In 1987, his operation, Swanton Berry Farm, became the first organically certified strawberry grower in California. Eleven years later, Swanton became the first organic farm to sign a contract with the UFW. Today Swanton Berry remains the only organic farm in the country to have a collective bargaining agreement with the farmworkers' union. "I like the union label, because it means that the workers are saying, 'It's OK,'" Cochran said.

The 30 workers at Swanton Berry—who earn between $9 and $11 an hour—have a medical plan, a pension plan, holiday pay, and subsidized housing in a pair of well-kept bunkhouses with a view of the Pacific. If they need a loan to cover emergency expenses, workers can get an advance on their paychecks. Once workers have put in 500 hours on the farm, they can begin buying stock in the company.

"Fair Made" Label

While Cochran's commitment to social justice is laudable, being a union farm makes his costs 15 percent higher than those of other organic growers. Because union certification seems unrealistic for the small and medium-sized farms that still make up the bulk of organic growers, a range of organizations is working on proposals to create some kind of "fair made" label to encourage farmers to adopt better labor policies.

At least half a dozen projects are in the works. The Rural Advancement Foundation International and the Farmworker Support Committee have enlisted five farms in a pilot project demonstrating best labor practices. Growers in Canada have started a "fair deal" label. The organic soap maker Dr. Bronner's is implementing fair-trade standards to "improve the livelihoods of farmers and workers," while some dairy farmers have come together under the Wisconsin Fair Trade cheese initiative.

The slew of different programs demonstrates an energetic grassroots commitment to improving worker treatment. But there is a danger that having too many separate standards will be confusing to consumers and cumbersome for growers. So the various interests have come together in an ad-hoc coalition—the Domestic Fair Trade Working Group—to develop a single set of labor standards, a single monitoring process for farms, and one seal that consumers can trust to mean workers were treated right. The draft principles include a living wage for farmworkers, fair prices for farmers, transparent business practices, and family farm ownership.

Coming Soon-ish to a Supermarket Near You

Of course, another alternative would be to try to amend the existing USDA organic seal to include labor standards. But with advocates already busy fighting back efforts by the major food processors to loosen the organic rules, creating an independent label appears the best way to go.

"The government can't lead on this," said Cecil Wright, director of local operations at Organic Valley, a cooperative of more than 800 family-owned dairies, ranches, and farms. "We need to have the people who know what they're doing, who are entrepreneurial, to lead. We believe that at some point in the future we'll need a standard that goes above and beyond the USDA label."

When will that point be? Participants in the coalition agree it will be at least three years before shoppers can expect to see an independent label that certifies decent working conditions. In the meantime, advocates point out that there are a number of steps farmers can take to make their employees feel more valued. A recent [in August 2006] report by the California Institute for Rural Studies looked at best labor practices on 12 organic farms and identified several low-cost ways for cash-strapped farmers to improve workplace conditions. When interviewed, farmworkers said a slower pace of work, year-round employment, free food from the farm, flexible schedules, and plain old "respectful treatment" would make them feel like their work was important.

The stakes are high when it comes to the successful creation of a "fair labor" organic seal, and the importance of the struggle goes beyond the tight-knit sustainable-food community. If organic farmers can find a way to produce food without exploiting either the environment or their workers, advocates say, they can set an example for other industries to follow.

"For me, the big issue is in terms of progressive movement-building," said Ronnie Cummins, director of the Organic Consumers Association. "It's time to dovetail the health, sustainability, and justice movements. The potential is incredible. But it's going to take some real, hard organizing."

Organizations to Contact

The editors have compiled the following list of organizations concerned with the issues debated in this book. The descriptions are derived from materials provided by the organizations. All have publications or information available for interested readers. The list was compiled on the date of publication of the present volume; the information provided here may change. Be aware that many organizations take several weeks or longer to respond to inquiries, so allow as much time as possible.

American Council on Science and Health (ACSH)
1995 Broadway, 2nd Fl., New York, NY   10023-5860
(212) 362-7044
e-mail: acsh@acsh.org
website: www.acsh.org

ACSH provides consumers with scientific evaluations of issues related to food, pharmaceuticals, chemicals, and the environment, pointing out both health hazards and benefits. Its representatives participate in a variety of government and media events, testifying at congressional hearings and appearing on television and radio news programs. Its website includes relevant articles and reports.

Cato Institute
1000 Massachusetts Ave. NW, Washington, DC   20001-5403
(202) 842-0200 • fax: (202) 842-3490
e-mail: cato@cato.org
website: www.cato.org

The Cato Institute is a libertarian public policy research foundation dedicated to limiting the role of government and protecting individual liberties. It asserts that the concern over the possible health risks of pesticide use in agriculture is overstated. The institute publishes the quarterly *Cato Journal*, the bimonthly *Cato Policy Report*, and numerous books and commentaries.

Center for Science in the Public Interest (CSPI)

1875 Connecticut Ave. NW, Suite 300, Washington, DC   20009
(202) 332-9110
e-mail: cspi@cspinet.org
website: www.cspinet.org

Formed in 1971, the Center for Science in the Public Interest (CSPI) is a nonprofit education and consumer advocacy organization dedicated to fighting for government food policies and corporate practices that promote healthy diets. CSPI also works to prevent deceptive marketing practices and ensures that science is used for public welfare. It publishes *Nutrition Action Healthletter*, the most widely circulated health newsletter in North America.

Cornucopia Institute

P.O. Box 126, Cornucopia, Wisconsin   54827
(608) 625-2042
e-mail: cultivate@cornucopia.org
website: www.cornucopia.org

The Cornucopia Institute's mission is to promote economic justice for family scale farming. It supports educational activities that spread the ecological and economic principles that underlay sustainable and organic agriculture. Through research and investigations on agricultural issues, the Cornucopia Institute provides information to consumers, family farmers, and the media about organic food and farming.

Food and Nutrition Service (FNS)

1400 Independence Avenue, S.W., Washington, DC   20250
(202) 720-2791
website: www.fns.usda.gov

The Food and Nutrition Service is an agency of the US Department of Agriculture (USDA) and is responsible for administering the nation's domestic nutrition assistance programs. It provides prepared meals, food assistance, and nutrition education materials to one in five Americans. The agency also encourages children and teens to follow the healthy eating guidelines set by MyPyramid in its "Eat Smart, Play Hard" campaign.

Food First: Institute for Food and Development Policy
398 60th St., Oakland, CA   94618
(510) 654-4400
website: www.foodfirst.org

Food First, founded by the author of *Diet for a Small Planet*, promotes sustainable agriculture and seeks to eliminate causes of hunger. Its current projects include the Cuban Organic Agriculture Exchange Program and Californians for Pesticide Reform. Its website includes articles and press releases as well as audio and video postings addressing its various initiatives.

Food Safety Consortium (FSC)
110 Agriculture Building, Fayetteville, AR   72701
(501) 575-5647
website: http://www.uark.edu/depts/fsc

Congress established the Food Safety Consortium (FSC), consisting of researchers from the University of Arkansas, Iowa State University, and Kansas State University, in 1988 through a special Cooperative State Research Service grant. The FSC conducts extensive investigation into all areas of poultry, beef, and pork meat production.

Friends of the Earth (FoE)
1717 Massachusetts Avenue, Washington, DC   20036
(202) 783-7400
e-mail: foe@foe.org
website: www.foe.org

Friends of the Earth monitors legislation and regulations that affect the environment. The group's Safer Food, Safer Farms Campaign speaks out against what it perceives as the negative impact biotechnology can have on farming, food production, genetic resources, and the environment.

Organic Agriculture and Products Education Institute (Organic Institute)

PO Box 547, Greenfield, MA 01302
website: www.theorganicinstitute.org

The Organic Institute was created by members of the Organic Trade Association (OTA). Its mission is to educate the public regarding the attributes, benefits, and practices of organic agriculture and products for better environmental and personal health. Its website offers a downloadable guide for students who want to bring organic dining to their school or college campus.

Organic Trade Association

P.O. Box 547, Greenfield, MA 01302
. (413) 774-7511
website: www.ota.com

The Organic Trade Association (OTA) is a membership-based business association that focuses on the organic business community in North America. OTA's mission is to promote and protect the growth of organic trade to benefit the environment, farmers, the public, and the economy.

Rodale Institute

611 Siegfriedale Road, Kutztown, PA 19530-9320
(610) 683-1400
e-mail: info@rodaleinst.org
website: www.rodaleinstitute.org

The Rodale Institute was founded in 1947 by organic pioneer J.I. Rodale. The Institute employs soil scientists and a cooperating network of researchers who assert that organic farming techniques offer the best solution to global warming and famine. Their website offers information on the longest-running US study comparing organic and conventional farming techniques, a study that forms the basis for Rodale's practical training to thousands of farmers in Africa, Asia, and the Americas.

US Environmental Protection Agency (EPA)
Ariel Rios Building, Washington, DC   20460
(202) 272-0167
website: www.epa.gov

The Environmental Protection Agency (EPA) is a government agency that, among other things, regulates pesticides under two major federal statutes. It establishes maximum legally permissible levels for pesticide residues in food, registers pesticides for use in the United States, and prescribes labeling and other regulatory requirements to prevent unreasonable adverse effects on health and the environment.

US Food and Drug Administration (FDA)
10903 New Hampshire Ave., Silver Spring, MD   20903
(888)INFO-FDA (888-463-6332)
website: www.fda.gov

The Food and Drug Administration (FDA) is a public health agency, charged with protecting American consumers by enforcing the Federal Food, Drug, and Cosmetic Act and several related public health laws. To carry out this mandate of consumer protection, FDA has investigators and inspectors cover the country's almost 95,000 FDA-regulated businesses. Its publications include government documents, reports, fact sheets, and press announcements.

Bibliography

Books

Alex Avery	*The Truth About Organic Foods.* Chesterfield, MO: Henderson Communications, 2006.
Denis Avery	*Saving the Planet with Pesticides and Plastic: The Environmental Triumph of High-Yield Farming.* Washington, DC: Hudson Institute, 2000.
Cindy Burke	*To Buy Or Not Buy Organic: What You Need to Know to Choose the Healthiest, Safest, Most Earth-Friendly Food.* New York: Da Capo, 2007.
Jeff Cox	*The Organic Cook's Bible.* Hoboken, NJ: Wiley & Sons, 2006.
Jeff Cox	*The Organic Food Shopper's Guide.* Hoboken, NJ: Wiley & Sons, 2008.
Tanya L. K. Denckla	*The Gardener's A-Z Guide to Growing Organic Food.* North Adams, MA: Storey, 2003.
Samuel Fromartz	*Organic Inc.: Natural Foods and How They Grew.* New York: Harcourt, 2006.
James McWilliams	*Just Food: Where Locavores Get It Wrong.* New York: Back Bay, 2009.

Joseph Mercola and Ben Lerner — *Generation XL: Raising Healthy, Intelligent Kids in a High-Tech, Junk-Food World*. Nashville, TN: Thomas Nelson, 2007.

Steve Meyerowitz — *The Organic Food Guide: How to Shop Smarter and Eat Healthier*. Guildford, CN: Globe Pequot, 2004.

Marion Nestle — *Food Politics: How the Food Industry Influences Nutrition and Health*. Los Angeles, CA: University of California, 2002.

Marion Nestle — *What to Eat*. New York: North Point, 2006.

Robert Paarlberg — *Food Politics: What Everyone Needs to Know*. New York: Oxford, 2010.

Luddene Perry and Dan Schultz — *A Field Guide to Buying Organic*. New York: Bantam, 2007.

Michael Pollan — *In Defense of Food: An Eater's Manifesto*. New York: Penguin, 2009.

Jill Richardson — *Recipe for America: Why Our Food System Is Broken and What We Can Do to Fix It*. Brooklyn, NY: Ig Publishing, 2009.

Michele Simon — *Appetite for Profit: How the Food Industry Undermines Our Health and How to Fight Back*. New York: Nation, 2006.

Karl Weber, editor   *Food Inc.: A Participant Guide: How Industrial Food Is Making Us Sicker, Fatter, and Poorer, and What You Can Do About It.* Philadelphia, PA: Public Affairs, 2009.

Periodicals

Glenn Baker   "Green Monkey See, Green Monkey Do," *NZ Business*, December 2009.

J. Steven Bird   "A Small Green Food Machine," *Natural Life*, July–August 2010.

Alan Borst   "Organic Farmers Increasingly Turn to Cooperative Business Model," *Rural Cooperatives*, May–June 2010.

Linda Buchwald   "Learning from Labels," *Scholastic Choices*, November–December 2009.

Claire Connors   "The Health That Got Me Fit," *Shape*, February 2009.

Corn & Soybean Digest   "Are Organic Foods Over-Hyped?" July 30, 2010.

James Delingpole   "Eat Local Organic Food If You Like, But Don't Kid Yourself That It's Green," *Spectator*, September 18, 2010.

Catherine Elton   "Home Delivery," *Time*, August 30, 2010.

Meagan Francis   "Healthy Eats for Kids," *Natural Health*, September 2009.

Julia M. Gallo-Torres	"Fortified Junk Food?" *Prepared Foods*, February 2009.
Just-Food	"Ethical Food: A Complicated Picture," September 13, 2010.
Jeffrey Kluger	"What's So Great About Organic Food?" *Time*, August 30, 2010.
Stephanie Liberatore	"Health Wise," *Science Teacher*, September 2008.
Alex MacEachern and Dan Zdzieborski	"Organically Entertaining: Having Company?" *Natural Life*, May–June 2010.
David Orgel	"Warning Signs for Organic/Natural in New Data?" *Supermarket News*, July 12, 2010.
Janet Oswald	"Planning for Urban Agriculture," *Plan Canada*, Summer 2009.
Josh Ozersky	"Farm vs. Supermarket," *Time*, August 30, 2010.
Mark Pendergrast	"Going Organic for Good," *Wine Spectator*, March 31, 2010.
Andrew Purvis	"The Organic Dilemma," *Grocer*, July 10, 2010.
Merritt Watts	"Ready, Set, Grow!" *Self*, April 2010.

Index